Advance Praise
for *College Admissions:*
The Essential Guide for Busy Parents

"Wow! This book is amazing! It feels like it's speaking directly to me (and I'm sure countless other parents in my exact position). Not only does it address so many of our specific concerns, it also lays out a step-by-step plan of action in a thoughtful and reassuring manner that gives direction and hope. This book is going to be invaluable for parents of students who are preparing for college, especially as this process seems more overwhelming and confusing than ever!"

—Alana McIntyre

"This book is a gem—practical stuff that all parents should have on hand as they navigate the college application process with their teen."

—Jessica Everton

"As the mother of a high school sophomore, this is going to be my world very soon. I learned so much in this book! It really breaks down the process and walks the reader through each phase. It was absolutely amazing to me that anyone could construct such a comprehensive guidebook considering all the seemingly disparate variables and deadlines (interviews, counseling, varying requirements, meetings, finances, résumés, essays, application portals). All the stuff that scares me to death!"

—Melinda Recchi

COLLEGE

ADMISSIONS

THE ESSENTIAL GUIDE FOR BUSY PARENTS

THE ESSENTIAL
GUIDE FOR
BUSY PARENTS

COLLEGE
ADMISSIONS

BETH PICKETT
FOUNDER OF COLLEGE PREP COUNSELING

MUSE
LITERARY

Published by Muse Literary

Copyright © 2022 by Beth Pickett, College Prep Counseling

ISBN Softcover: 978-1-949550-87-0
ISBN Hardcover: 978-1-949550-89-4
Ebook ISBN: 978-1-949550-90-0

Visit the College Prep Counseling website at CollegePrepCounseling.com

Join the book's Facebook Group:
https://www.facebook.com/groups/admissionessentials

Disclaimer: The author believes the information in this book to be accurate at the time of publishing. The information contained in this book is provided for general information and educational purposes, and is not, nor is it intended to be, legal or financial advice.

ACT® is a registered trademark of ACT, Inc., which is not affiliated with, and does not endorse, this publication.

Advanced Placement®, BigFuture®, CSS Financial Aid Profile®, and SAT® are trademarks registered by the College Board, which is not affiliated with, and does not endorse, this publication.

FAFSA® is a registered trademark of the U.S. Department of Education.

International Baccalaureate® and IB® are trademarks registered by the International Baccalaureate Organization, which is not affiliated with, and does not endorse, this publication.

PSAT/NMSQT® is a registered trademark of the College Board and the National Merit Scholarship Corporation, which are not affiliated with, and do not endorse, this publication.

Table of Contents

Introduction

I t's hard to believe that the years have flown by and it's already time for your high schooler to be thinking about college applications. You remember from your own experience, or you've heard from your friends, that the application process can be complicated, overwhelming, and stressful. Today, getting accepted at selective four-year colleges—for the purposes of this book, those that accept fewer than 60% of applicants—is more competitive and more cumbersome than it was back in the day. Many colleges have become tremendously more popular (and therefore more difficult to get into) than they were even 20 years ago. Duke's admission rate is down to 7.8%, Bowdoin's is 9.2%, and USC's is 16.1%. The landscape has changed, and parents who don't realize that may be in for a shock. Misjudging the college landscape may also result in their student creating a wholly unrealistic college list that leaves them with very few choices come spring of their senior year.

This guide is for you if you want your student to be in the driver's seat, but you also want to be able to offer good advice, keep tabs on where they are in the process, and know that they're on schedule so you can offer support in case they veer off track. You want to know what they should be doing, and when, so you can answer their questions and guide them as needed.

You also know that you are at least partially—if not fully—on the hook for the financial piece of this equation, and that America's private colleges can run $80,000 or more per year for those paying the full amount. Luckily, that is not the majority of families—I'll explain why in the financial aid section. As much as we want our teens to tackle this endeavor on their own, college today is just too expensive to go into the application process without understanding the financial implications that should help shape the list of colleges to which your student will be applying. Remember: you may need to write a four- or five-figure check each semester for four or more years. Going through the application process with clarity and intention—specifically, helping your teen carefully consider which colleges make it onto their final list—can help you make informed decisions that will lower those costs or at least let you go in with your eyes wide open.

Ideally, supporting your student through the college admissions process will be an opportunity to connect with your teen in a positive way rather than defaulting to the Badger-in-Chief role, nagging them for the next several months about getting essays written or forms completed. This book will give you a solid understanding of the many components of a college application and how and when the student should request, gather, or create those materials.

In this book, I'll walk you through the key components of a college application, pointing you to resources, best practices, and a timeline for completing each task. You deserve to have this clearly spelled out so you and your student can work together to make good choices at every step, avoid mistakes, and not feel as though you are lost or floundering.

I'll also show you what an ideal timeline looks like for getting the applications done with the least amount of stress, and I'll clarify the factors to consider as you support and collaborate with your student in making decisions along the way. This book is a tool to take you step-by-step down the critical path and help you understand core considerations at each juncture, all while breaking the overall task into manageable, bite-sized chunks to eliminate deadline stress and application overwhelm for you or for your teen. Everything is organized in one place for quick reference so you don't have to spend hours sifting through random pages on the internet that may or may not give you accurate information.

Who am I to be walking you through this? I'm Beth Pickett, a college admissions professional who has been helping students and families with this process since 2007. I graduated from Stanford University and earned a certificate in College Counseling from UCLA. I've worked with students from the country's top public and private high schools and helped students earn admission to their best-fit colleges. For some, that meant an Ivy League university. For others, that meant a state or community college—which one student chose to attend despite an offer of admission from a University of California school, as she was self-aware enough to realize what the best option was for her mental health. I'm also the mother of two teenage boys—so I get it.

Some families are surprised by how many hours of work go into researching colleges, writing essays, and preparing and submitting applications. As one of my client moms said recently, "I just can't believe what a circus they've made out of applying to a college! Back in my day, we just did it! Fill out the application, write an essay, send in the scores, bam. Now it's a whole new scene."

I've found that the best way to guide students through the process is to help them get a head start, preferably in spring of their junior year of high school. Working on their apps at a slow and steady pace can prevent breakdowns, freak-outs, exasperation, and exhaustion on your part and on the part of the student.

This process can also be stressful for families because it happens to fall at precisely the time when students are seeking more independence from their parents and often make a concerted effort to dismiss parental advice and guidance. Beware if your student says, "I've got this" when, in fact, they haven't "got this" at all. Encourage them to share their lists, strategies, and evidence that they are getting the work done. And keep in mind as this process unfolds that now is a good time to let your student know that they are accomplished and can be successful in life regardless of the admissions decision of any single college. Reassure them that you love them no matter what.

Are you ready to get a clearer picture of how this process works and how you can support your student on this journey? If so, then let's go!

1

The College Search: Start with the Student

As parents, we want the best for our children. We will do most anything to help set them up for happy, independent futures. For many of us, this includes plans to send them off to college. We dream of launching them into a school where they can learn, mature, build their skills at "adulting," and graduate with a degree that can help them kick off a career, not just get a job. Too often, though, parents and students struggle to know where to begin their college search. There are nearly 3,000 public and private four-year colleges in the United States. Your student should anticipate applying to between 10 and 16 of them. How are you supposed to help them winnow down that list?

Many students start by listing schools where family and friends have graduated, big-name colleges in the Ivy League, or those that are familiar names because they consistently do well in the March Madness NCAA basketball tournament. It's also quite common for parents to grab a copy of *U.S. News and World Report* to check their college rankings.

I recommend a more methodical approach that starts with the student. Define the factors that the student is looking for in their college experience. What does the student want to study? Do they prefer discussion-based seminar classes or lectures? Do they do their best in a competitive atmosphere, or would their academics benefit from collaboration and cooperative projects? Do they want access to a lot of outdoorsy activities, or would they prefer to be in a city environment? Are they eager to join a fraternity/sorority, or just as eager to avoid those—or do they not have a preference either way? Is racial, geographic, or socioeconomic diversity among the students important to them? Defining the parameters that are most important to the student helps them create an individualized list of colleges that align with those preferences.

Approaching the college list in this way lets the student know that they are the priority and get to take the lead. It ensures they know *why* they are applying to the schools they've selected for their list and relieves the pressure valve of getting into a handful of highly ranked, highly selective (also known as "highly rejective") schools that may not even offer the programs, services, or environment where the student could thrive.

One of my students was second in his class in his large suburban high school. He had a spectacular grade point average (GPA) of 4.6 and crushed his standardized tests, and he had strong and unique extracurricular activities. He could have been a viable candidate at any school in the country. But he wasn't interested in most of the big-name schools. He wanted a place where he could study environmental science and art in a beautiful setting with great access to the outdoors, so he limited his search to liberal arts colleges in the Pacific Northwest. His final college list reflected those specific college factors that were important to him. He chose colleges that met his criteria, rather than letting the rankings do that for him.

WHAT DOES THE STUDENT WANT TO STUDY?

As we begin to narrow the list from those 3,000 four-year colleges, the first order of business is to help the student figure out what they think they may want to study. Some students already have a strong sense of this. Others feel completely in the dark, but when they stop to consider their favorite academic subjects and what they like to spend time doing, ideas may emerge.

For my students who say they have no idea what they might like to study, I send them an assessment from YouScience. com. (It's also available for direct purchase for about $30 from their website.) That assessment asks the student to complete a series of about eight tasks, called "brain games," to tease out information about how their brain is wired. It then matches the student's results to various careers best suited to their brain wiring. It gives students a starting point to launch the discussion.

Note that all we are doing here is helping the student find a general direction they might like to follow through college. We are not asking them to commit to a career field for the next 40 years. The key is to make sure that the student finds a college that offers the academic subjects and programs they'd be excited to study. For example, if we know that a student is more aligned toward engineering than English, we'll immediately know that schools that don't offer engineering are off the list. Students who have a very specific interest such as turfgrass management (according to one school's website for that department, "Love sports and working outdoors? Become an expert in the science of maintaining golf courses, sports fields, and more") would immediately be able to narrow their lists to the five U.S. colleges that offer that major.

If a student wants to go through the college search as "undecided," that is okay, too, as long as they find a school with enough subject offerings of interest that they feel they'd be able to eventually find a major. Yes, most colleges offer a variety of subjects, but some are very specific. For example, every graduate of Soka University of America earns a B.A. in Liberal Arts; students at St. John's College—either the Maryland or New Mexico campuses—study the Great Books and, like at Soka, all earn one degree: a B.A. in Liberal Arts.

For many colleges, the open spots in certain majors such as engineering, computer science, business, film, and nursing fill up with students applying directly into those programs out of high school, so transferring in once the student has started college may not be an option. Students should check the rules of transferring from one major to another for each school on their list so that they know ahead of time what is and is not an option.

WHAT COLLEGE CHARACTERISTICS DOES THE STUDENT WANT?

Next, determine the criteria the student wants in a college. You can think of these criteria as a sort of à la carte menu of choices that the student gets to pick from as they consider what's important to them in their college experience. There are no right or wrong answers to these; it's simply a matter of preference on the part of the student. I've listed some of the key criteria below.

Geography. Is the student considering only colleges in the United States, or are they (and you) open to looking at colleges in Canada, Europe, or Asia? If in the United States, would the student consider a college in Arkansas or Alaska? Or only in the Northeast? Does the student want to attend college within a certain number of miles from home?

Location. Does the student want to be in the middle of a city with all its bustling activities beyond what the campus offers, with internship possibilities and people of all ages weaving through their daily lives? Or perhaps they want a more suburban campus setting, where most of their activities and interactions will be campus-based with students of their own age, and where street-smarts and city issues are less of a concern? Maybe the student is more comfortable in a rural setting, where the campus is really the only game in town for activities and peer interactions.

Climate. Is your student okay with a long, snowy winter or are they hoping to study in a sunny part of the country? Or is climate not one of their critical college criteria?

Student population size. Does your student want to attend a very small college of fewer than 2,000 students, a small college with 2,000–5,000 students, a medium-sized college with 5,000–10,000 students, a large college with 10,000–20,000 students, or an extra-large college with more than 20,000 students? Smaller colleges typically offer seminar-style classes (students and the professor gathered around a table discussing the topic of the day) for all four years. Larger campuses will often have lecture-style courses of 100 students or more for core classes in the student's freshman and sophomore years. At smaller colleges, students will likely get to know the majority of other students on campus and may get to know their professors quite well; at larger colleges, they'll have their group of friends but will constantly be encountering new faces and may need to make an extra effort to get to know faculty members.

Campus Facilities. Does the student want a campus that is clearly delineated (that is, you know when you step onto campus versus when you are not on campus)? Or is the student fine with a college that has buildings loosely scattered across a town or city? Is it important to have the grassy quad and ivy-covered buildings? Does the student need special on-campus meal options such as vegan, gluten-free, kosher, etc.? What about a well-appointed gym where students can work out to relieve stress and stay healthy?

Campus Culture. Are the students at a particular college super brainy, thriving on discussing intellectual topics deep into the night? Or do most students "work hard, play hard," setting aside academics over the weekends to go have fun? Is the campus composed of very religious students of mostly one faith or another, or is religion not a key aspect of the university? Is the campus LGBTQ-friendly, and does this matter to the student? Are racial and socioeconomic diversity among the student body important to the student? Are the students at the college competitive with one another for top grades, or is there more of a sense of cooperation and collaboration? Is there a strong emphasis on community service on campus, and does that align with what your student values? Are the students on campus seeking intellectual growth for the sake of learning, or are they focused on what they need to learn to launch their careers—or some combination of those? What is the general attitude of students and what is the atmosphere on campus?

Athletics. For some students, attending big football games and cheering for the home team is a central part of their image of what it means to be a college student. Others don't care whether there's a sports culture on campus. Some want to be able to play their sport on an intercollegiate team or at least participate in intramural sports.

Greek life. Some students are eager to join a fraternity or sorority; other students are just as eager to avoid joining a fraternity or sorority. Some could take it or leave it. Either way, it's important to know what the role of Greek life is on each campus and whether that aligns with the student's ideal options for their social life.

Academic fit. Is your student likely to be one of the top students at the college or are they more likely to be in the middle of the pack? If they have plans for medical school or law school, having a high college GPA will be a critical part of those applications, so it's a good idea to consider where the student can challenge themselves without drowning in the academic workload.

Among these, which are most important to the student, and which are less important? For example, is the location within 200 miles from home a more important criteria for that student than whether or not there is strong Greek life? Prioritizing these parameters will help define the student's list.

To help think through some of these factors with your student, I offer a free printable sheet you can access at https://www.CollegePrepCounseling.com/resources/.

PLUG THE FACTORS INTO A COLLEGE SEARCH DATABASE

Once you have a clear idea of what the student wants to study (or have determined that the student will apply undecided) and what criteria are important to them in a college, you can head to a college search database to come up with a list of colleges.

With my clients, I enter their criteria and preferences into software specifically designed for college counselors to use with their students, and we keep refining or expanding the search until we come up with 25 to 40 colleges the student can then begin to research in-depth. Clients in my online courses also have access to this software and can enter their criteria to run the searches.

If you and your student are tackling this on your own, there are a few free college search engines out there that you might find helpful.

BigFuture® from the College Board® (collegesearch.collegeboard.org/home) lets you search by major, location, type of school, or campus life. Once you've done a search based on one of those options, you can layer on other criteria to refine the search.

Cappex (Cappex.com) has a filter that I find easy to navigate. It starts with student population size, major, and location. I like that it also offers a way to sort by net price (the average that families pay after financial aid) rather than solely on sticker price. I'll cover these critical considerations—finances and cost—in more depth in the next chapter.

College Navigator from NCES, the National Center for Education Statistics (https://nces.ed.gov/collegenavigator/), is a helpful tool even if the user interface looks like it hasn't been updated since the turn of the millennium. Be sure to click "more search options" on the left-hand navigation bar to open up the choices for school population size, percent of applicants admitted, and more. And leave the zip code option blank unless you only want to see colleges within 250 miles or fewer of that zip code, or you can specify the miles in the "miles from" pull-down menu to the right of the zip-code entry. Particularly useful on this site, once you drill down to a specific college, is the "net price" information broken down by family income bands. In other words, what's the average amount that families in your income bracket pay out of pocket for a student to attend that school?

Then there are the printed guidebooks, notably the annual *Fiske Guide to Colleges* and a less-well-known but incredibly helpful book, *Colleges Worth Your Money: A Guide to What America's Top Schools Can Do for You.*

I recommend to my students that they track college information using a spreadsheet that lists the college name, the city and state where it's located, whether it's a public or private institution, the undergraduate and total student population size, the most recent acceptance rate, the middle range SAT® or ACT® assessment scores, and the four-year graduation rate.

You can save yourself hours of work by downloading the free version of this spreadsheet that my team has pre-filled with this information for about 200 of the most popular colleges in the U.S. You can access it at https://www.CollegePrepCounseling.com/resources.

The college's four-year graduation rate is the percentage of students who finish their degree within four years. Although this is a critical number, colleges often only make their six-year graduation rate easy to find. But I don't want any of my clients to take *six years* to graduate. I want to know what percentage of students are finishing in four years (which is why it's included in my pre-filled spreadsheet). You can also find this on your own with a Google search (for example, "Oberlin College four-year graduation rate") or by looking at the college's Common Data Set, which I'll discuss in more detail in the next chapter. If a college on the list has less than a 50% four-year graduation rate, then I'd want the student to have an extremely compelling reason why that college should stay on the list.

The student's goal for this first pass should be to come up with 25 to 40 colleges that they will then investigate further to see which might land on their final list of 10 to 16 colleges.

KEEP AN OPEN MIND

The perfect college for your student may be one you've never heard of, so try to keep an open mind. College awareness tends to be somewhat regional, with families knowing about big-name colleges around the country but being less familiar with colleges that are out of their area. One student in Maine accepted an admissions offer from the California Institute of Technology (Caltech). Her friends expressed disappointment because they assumed she'd go to MIT and that Caltech "must not be good because we've never heard of it." They simply didn't know that Caltech is every bit as amazing as MIT, and, for this student, it was a better fit.

One of my California students was set on studying entrepreneurship, so I suggested Babson, a college of about 3,000 students in Massachusetts that focuses on business and entrepreneurship. At first, the family wasn't open to that option because they had never heard of it, but after more research, it became a top choice. I've had a similar response from other families when I recommended Carleton College. It's a fabulous school in Minnesota that most of my East Coast and West Coast families don't know much about (I consider it a hidden gem).

There are several other places you can look to learn more about colleges you've never heard of. The website Niche.com offers a familiar letter-grading system (A through F) for a college's academics, diversity, athletics, campus, party scene, and overall value. And it has a place where current students can discuss what they think are the pros and cons of their school.

If you're looking for more objective data, Georgetown University's Center on Education and the Workforce website (https://cew.georgetown.edu/cew-reports/CollegeROI/) looks at the return on investment (ROI) at 4,500 colleges and universities in the U.S. This, however, is largely based on financial and salary information from graduates, which is only one aspect to consider when evaluating a college.

CollegeNet offers a Social Mobility Index (https://www.socialmobilityindex.org/) that "focuses directly on the factors that enable economic mobility," according to their website. "To what extent does a college or university educate more economically disadvantaged people ... at lower tuition so that they graduate into good paying jobs? The colleges that do best at this rank higher according to the SMI [Social Mobility Index]." Criteria include the percent of the student population that is low income, the graduation score, the median early career salary, the average debt per graduate, and more. Colleges are listed by SMI from a high of 379 to a low of zero.

KEY TAKEAWAYS

1) Start with the student, not with a list of school rankings.
2) Help the student figure out their college priorities—the subject or area they want to study and the criteria that are important to them. Check the four-year graduation rate. Use those factors to winnow down the list to 25 to 40 colleges.
3) Keep an open mind. A school you haven't heard of may turn out to be the perfect fit for your student.

2

The Role of Finances

Once your student has come up with that list of 25 to 40 colleges, it's time to look at the financial picture more closely. I'd like you to determine, right at the outset before the student's college list is finalized, which of those schools is reasonably affordable for your family once need-based financial aid and average merit aid scholarships are taken into account. If a college's cost is going to put off your retirement for an extra 10 or 20 years, or it's going to saddle your student with loans until they are in their 40s, get that college off the student's list right now, before they ever send in an application.

I cannot emphasize enough how important it is for parents to understand the basics of how financial aid works and then have the student apply only to those colleges that make financial sense for your family. This is more complicated than simply looking at the cost of tuition or even the all-in "sticker price" of a college. The amount you end up paying comes down to each college's financial aid and merit aid offer *for your individual student*, not the published cost of attendance.

My sister told me a story from her small East Coast town where a mom asked on Facebook, in the summer before her twins headed off to college, whether anyone knew of a good bank for a college loan. That family had apparently not thought about how they would pay for their sons' education until three months before the boys left for campus, and now they were in panic mode. I absolutely do not want that to happen to you.

I am neither a Certified Public Accountant nor a Certified Financial Planner, but I will do my best to explain the basics of how financial aid works. I recommend that you consult with a college financial aid expert to get custom advice on this process (few traditional CPAs and CFPs know the nuanced ins and outs of college financial aid). I've found that knowledgeable advisors can often save families 10 times or more the cost of their services—and they can fill out the headache-inducing financial aid forms for the family, or at least double-check the work to help families avoid common mistakes.

In any case, most parents take one of two paths when thinking about finances as they relate to paying for their teen's college education: the "Sticker Shock" path or the "We'll Find a Way" path. But both of these can lead to decades of excess debt, delayed retirement, and missed opportunities for significant free money from colleges.

STICKER SHOCK

In the first path, parents look at the sticker-price cost of attending a college and, if the amount is out of their reach, they simply decide the student should not apply. The sticker price, also known as the "Cost of Attendance" (COA), is the full cost of sending a student to that college for one semester or one year. It includes not only tuition and fees, but housing and food (typically called room and board), student activity fees, books, transportation, and more. It's the all-in cost of sending a student to that college. You can find this number for any given college by doing an internet search such as "Lafayette College Cost of Attendance" or "Chapman University Cost of Attendance." Here's a summary of what I found during a quick online search for Chapman's COA:

Cost of Attendance Breakdown

Tuition and fees based on full-time enrollment of 12 to 18 credits. Additional charges will apply for students enrolled in more than 18 credits a semester. Health insurance is not automatically included in the Cost of Attendance.

2022-2023 Undergraduate Cost of Attendance				
		With Parents or Relatives	Off Campus	On Campus	On Campus: First-Time Freshman
Tuition Fees		$ 60,288	$ 60,288	$ 60,288	$ 60,288
	Wellness Center	$ 244	$ 244	$ 244	$ 244
	Associated Student Body Fee	$ 140	$ 140	$ 140	$ 140
Books and Supplies		$ 1,600	$ 1,600	$ 1,600	$ 1,600
Room		$ 4,266	$ 10,640	$ 13,876	$ 11,362
Board		$ 2,466	$ 3,884	$ 5,592	$ 5,592
Personal		$ 2,000	$ 2,000	$ 2,000	$ 2,000
Transportation		$ 2,000	$ 2,000	$ 1,250	$ 1,250
Loan fees		$ 70	$ 70	$ 70	$ 70
Total		$ 73,074	$ 80,866	$ 85,060	$ 82,546

Parents who see the bottom line $73,000–$82,000 per year total cost may think, "We can't pay that," and steer their student to a college with a less-expensive sticker price. But wait! It very well could be that some private universities might end up significantly less expensive for that family, and perhaps even less expensive than a state college, after financial aid is taken into consideration. That's the piece that many families miss—a lot of students who would qualify for financial assistance end up not applying to the schools that could help them the most.

WE'LL FIND A WAY

The second path families sometimes take is the "Apply anywhere you like, and we will find a way to make it work." They think that sending their student to the "best" college will be worth taking out tens of thousands of dollars in loans, as long as it offers their child the opportunity to go to a college that they feel will help launch them into a successful career. This can lead to years of debt and putting off significant life events such as retiring (for the parents) or purchasing a home or starting a family (for the student).

Pro Tip

Everyone should fill out the forms to apply for financial aid, even families that think their income is so high there is no way they'll qualify. Why? If something happens to the family income (such as COVID shutdowns or an unexpected illness, death, or disability in the family), the student will already be in the financial aid system so their situation can be reviewed for an adjustment. In addition, at some colleges, students won't be considered for merit aid—that is, free money whether or not the family needs the help—if they didn't turn in the basic financial aid forms. I've seen families with no financial need walk away with more than $100,000 of merit scholarship money for their student over four years. Who wouldn't want that?

THE WORST MISTAKES

Students need to understand how critical it is, if they start college and borrow money, to *finish* college and earn their degree. Some of the worst college-cost-related financial situations arise when students start college, go into debt to pay for it, and then don't finish their degree. They still have to pay back the debt, but they don't get the paycheck boost that can come with a college diploma.

The second worst mistake is for the student to meander through college, changing majors so often that they can't complete their degree in four years, while the costs and the debt continue to pile on. A good rule of thumb: make sure your student understands that their goal is to graduate on time with as little debt as possible.

Another rule of thumb, this one from financial aid expert Mark Kantrowitz, is: the student should never borrow more for their undergraduate degree than they think they will make in their first year working. For example, if a student plans on becoming a teacher with a starting salary of $45,000 per year, then they shouldn't borrow more than $45,000 to pay for four years of college.

Another pitfall to avoid: Some colleges, particularly state colleges, have abysmal four-year graduation rates, where only 15% to 50% of students who start as freshmen graduate in four years. This leads families to pay for extra years of college for the student to earn their bachelor's degree and essentially wipes out any savings they might have realized by attending a state school with a less-expensive sticker price.

Also, don't let your student forget to find out which of their colleges accept credit for Advanced Placement®, International Baccalaureate®, and dual-enrollment courses taken in high school. I've worked with many students who used credit from these types of courses to essentially start college with sophomore standing and then graduate in three years. That can save an entire year of tuition, room, board, and other expenses.

THE RIGHT WAY TO CRUNCH THE NUMBERS

There really *is* a right way to crunch the numbers for college costs, but it takes a bit of determination and detective work to figure out. Given that it could save you tens or even hundreds of thousands of dollars over the course of four years of your student's education, it's well worth putting in the time to run the calculations. Think of it this way: If you spend 20 hours digging into these calculations to help shape your student's college list and that student ends up saving $80,000 over four years, then, in essence, you've been paid $4,000 per hour for spending that time doing the investigating. Whoo hoo!

One of my families whose income was over $200,000 per year did this, shaping a list where their student was not only pretty much a slam dunk for admission (his grades and test scores were much higher than those of the average admitted student), but where we knew he would qualify for a lot of scholarships. He was admitted to all the schools to which he applied and now attends a college where he's getting a $55,000-per-year merit scholarship, making the cost of his private college about the same as it would have been for him to attend his state college.

CALCULATING YOUR STUDENT'S FINANCIAL NEED AT A SPECIFIC COLLEGE

I've shown you how to find the Cost of Attendance at any particular college (search "Cost of Attendance" with the college name). Next, search for "Net Price Calculator" or "Net Cost Calculator" with the college name. These are website forms that allow you to estimate the net cost of that college for your family. They will often ask for your student's GPA, year in school, whether the student is first-generation (students whose parents did not earn a college degree), the age of the student, and the parents' income as reported on their taxes for the most recent year.

Most will ask for the income and assets of the parent or parents *and* the income and assets of the student (if any). Assets include checking, savings, cash, 529 college savings accounts in the student's or parents' names, mutual funds, stocks, trusts, and investment property. When the calculator asks for your total assets, *do not* include the equity in your primary residence or the value of your retirement accounts among your assets unless the calculator form specifically asks for those.

Entering all this information will generate an estimate (not a final offer) of what you can expect your financial aid package to look like at that college. "Self-help aid" means either loans or work-study (where the student finds a job on campus to help offset costs). You are looking for the "Estimated Net Cost," which is the best estimate of what your family would have to pay out of pocket to send your student to that college for one year (or one semester, depending on how the calculator is set up).

That is the number you should use when deciding whether a particular college is affordable for your family.

THE FAFSA®: FREE APPLICATION FOR FEDERAL STUDENT AID

The main form that families need to fill out to determine their eligibility for financial aid is called the FAFSA®—the Free Application for Federal Student Aid. Families can begin to fill out the FAFSA® starting October 1 of the student's senior year (although you should be aware of what's in it and how to plan for it well before then). You can find the FAFSA® website by searching "FAFSA Application" on the internet. Be careful, though; make sure the website you find has a ".gov" and not a ".com" name to ensure it's the correct site.

Filling out the FAFSA® generates something called the Student Aid Report, and in that report is a critical piece of information called the SAI, or "Student Aid Index." The SAI is the amount that the federal government thinks your family can afford to contribute, annually, to your child's college education. Unfortunately, most families are dismayed and astounded at their SAI, which they see as much higher than they can actually afford. In 2022, changes to the FAFSA® included renaming the SAI, which used to be called the EFC (or "Expected Family Contribution"). You may still see "EFC" used on college portals. Just know that it's the same as the SAI.

In my online financial aid course, I walk parents through the specifics of what assets the FAFSA® does and does not take into consideration. In some cases, families can legally and ethically move their assets from a category that is included on the FAFSA® into a category that is not taken into consideration, thereby potentially lowering their SAI and helping them qualify for more need-based aid.

For divorced or separated couples, it used to be that the family reported the income and assets of the parent who had greater custody. But the policy is changing with the FAFSA® forms for the academic year 2023–2024 (that is, the forms that the parents of students in the Class of 2023 will be filling out in October of 2022). The forms now ask the family to report the income and assets of the parent who contributes the most money to support the student, whether or not that parent has more custody.

The SAI is only the starting point for financial aid. Each college will take the SAI and run it through their own calculations to determine what institutional aid it will offer and how much the college will cost your individual family.

THE CSS FINANCIAL AID PROFILE®

About 250 colleges, including some of the nation's most selective schools (those with a 20% or lower admission rate), have decided that the information on the FAFSA® is insufficient. They want more, and they get that by requiring that families fill out a second financial aid form called the CSS Financial Aid Profile®—*in addition to* the FAFSA®. This profile looks even more closely at the family's finances (including retirement accounts and the equity in the family home, two factors that are not looked at in the FAFSA®). This greater detail can be helpful if the family has, for example, significant medical expenses for an elderly grandparent who lives in the home.

However, the extra information reported on the CSS Financial Aid Profile® can be problematic for some families, particularly for students whose parents do not live together and are separated, divorced, or were never married. For these families, most public colleges (those that ask only for the FAFSA®)

require only *one* parent's income and assets on the financial aid paperwork. If the parents are married or live together, they need to report both.

The majority of CSS Financial Aid Profile® colleges, however, also want to know the income and assets of the second parent, and this can completely change the financial aid picture for a student whose parents are no longer together. Searching "CSS Financial Aid Profile® Schools" on the web will show you a list of schools that require these forms.

For many of my client families where the student's parents are no longer together, the cost of attending one of the CSS Financial Aid Profile® schools that requires reporting of the non-custodial parent's finances is much higher. Why? Because it bases the financial aid calculations on two parent incomes and two sets of parental assets instead of one parent's income and assets. In some cases, those colleges are so much more expensive that my clients simply take them off the list right at the outset.

Unfortunately, colleges that require the CSS Financial Aid Profile® include all the Ivy League schools, plus many other highly ranked private colleges. If you are divorced or separated and both you and your ex-spouse have income and/or assets, then the price tag will likely be much higher at these schools than if your student applied to colleges that factor in only one parent's income and assets. Run the calculations and then you can decide whether you think those colleges are worth that extra cost. (Remember: this is for separated or divorced parents only; married parents—or those who live together regardless of marital status—need to report their dual income and assets no matter what.)

About a third of the 242 CSS Financial Aid Profile® colleges *do not* require information from the non-custodial parent.

You can search those on the CSS Financial Aid Profile® listing page by finding the column "CSS Profile—Noncustodial Parent" at the top of the page and setting the pull-down menu to "no." (If you don't see those pull-down menus on the page, try using a different browser such as Chrome.)

Bottom line: separated, divorced, or never-married parents should research each college to find out whether only one parent's income and assets need to be reported or both parents' incomes and assets need to be reported. If the family's expected contribution, after need-based aid and merit-based aid are estimated, is out of reach when both incomes are included, then those colleges that require reporting of both should be taken off the student's list.

Pro Tip

If you are thinking of getting remarried (or your ex-spouse is), the new spouse's income and assets become fair game for inclusion in the financial aid calculations. Remember, if the student's parents are separated or divorced or were never married and don't live together, then, on the FAFSA®, only *one* of those parents needs to report their income and assets. If that parent remarries, then that new spouse's income and assets must also be reported. It doesn't matter whether or not the new spouse wants to contribute or whether they have signed a prenup that states that the new parent won't contribute. The new spouse is not, of course, *obligated* to contribute, but their income and assets will be taken into account and that could alter the financial aid picture for the student.

PARENTAL REFUSAL TO PARTICIPATE

What if you, as the parent, simply state that you don't want to pay for your student's college costs—does that mean the student will qualify for more aid? Nope. Whether or not you choose to help finance your student's education is irrelevant to the colleges. They'll calculate the financial aid offer assuming that you will help, and if you choose not to, then your student will need to come up with another way to pay that share of the costs.

NEED-BASED AID

All these financial aid forms help the colleges determine whether you can fully pay their cost of attendance, or if there is a difference between the college costs and what your SAI says you can afford. That difference is your "need" at each individual college. And this is where we find that some private colleges may in fact turn out to be less expensive than some public colleges. Here's how it works.

Let's say a family in California has an SAI of $25,000, and the student is applying to UC Davis, Cal State University Channel Islands (CSUCI), Georgia Tech (a public school in Georgia for which this student will need to pay extra tuition as an out-of-state student), and Rensselaer Polytechnic Institute (RPI—a private college in Troy, New York). The calculation is basically "Cost of Attendance minus SAI = amount of need for that family."

COA minus SAI = Amount of Need				
	UC Davis	CSUCI	Georgia Tech	RPI
COA	$37,604	$27,952	$50,610	$77,763
EFC (SAI)	$25,000	$25,000	$25,000	$25,000
Need:	$12,604	$2,952	$25,610	$52,763

In other words, the family has a "need" of $12,604 of financial help to afford UC Davis; $2,952 of help to attend CSUCI; $25,610 of help to attend Georgia Tech; and $52,763 of help to attend RPI. That's their *need* at each school.

Here's the kicker, though. If CSUCI were to meet that $2,952 need by offering a loan, while RPI were to offer a full scholarship for $52,763, then suddenly the $77,000 private college would end up costing that family less than the public college. And that is why it's a mistake to only look at the Cost of Attendance. Granted, a full scholarship from RPI is highly unlikely, but the family's SAI—here, $25,000 per year—is the same regardless of the Cost of Attendance for each school, and the out-of-pocket costs for the family boil down to the specific financial aid offers from each college.

If a different family had an SAI of $100,000, then their "need" at any of these four schools would be zero. They would not qualify for any need-based aid because their SAI is higher than the Cost of Attendance at each of these schools.

MERIT-BASED AID

Merit-based aid is the other significant type of aid offered by many colleges, and it has nothing to do with the family income or assets (and is often not included in the net-price calculators). Merit-based aid, as the name implies, is based on merit. A student might be offered a merit scholarship at a college simply to entice that student to enroll at that university. Why would a college offer that? Either the student's high GPA and/or test scores will help raise the average at the college (thereby helping nudge it up in the college rankings game), or the college is hoping to encourage full-pay students to enroll by essentially offering them a discount in the form of merit aid. Athletic and performing arts scholarships are another type of merit aid that can be offered to students.

Note, however, that not all colleges offer merit aid. In particular, the eight Ivy League colleges do not offer one dime of merit money to any student. They are *very* generous with their need-based aid (in fact, most don't include any loans in their financial aid packages), so for high-need students who get accepted, it's an amazing bargain. But higher-income families who are hoping that merit aid might help offset the costs of an Ivy League education will be disappointed.

THE COMMON DATA SET

How do you know if the colleges your student is considering will offer merit aid (and, if they do, how generous they might be)? You check section H2A of the Common Data Set. Yes, I just saw your eyes glaze over. Stick with me while we wade through the weeds, as this is the part that may help you decide whether a college should make it onto your student's final list!

Almost all colleges report their core admissions statistics in a data bank called the Common Data Set. It's a treasure trove of information about each college and their admissions practices. You can usually find the Common Data Set for any college by simply doing an internet search of the college's name and "Common Data Set." These reports are updated annually, so try to find the most recent version. To make your search even easier, my team has created a financial aid spreadsheet that not only includes a direct link to the Common Data Set for nearly 200 colleges, but is pre-populated with columns indicating whether the college is public or private, which financial aid forms they require, the average merit aid award amount, and the percent of students who are offered merit aid for those colleges. You can access that spreadsheet through this book's resources at https://www.CollegePrepCounseling.com/resources.

Let's look at an example. Each college's Common Data Set follows a standard format, starting with sections A, B, C, and so on. The financial aid data is found in section H. Section H2 gives numbers for need-based aid (number of students who applied, number of students who were found to actually have need, number of students whose need was fully met, etc.).

The merit aid section is found in section H2, part A, which gives details about the "Number of enrolled students awarded non-need-based scholarships and grants"—that's merit aid! The numbers will be different for each college, but here's an example of how it looks:

H2A   Number of Enrolled Students Awarded Non-need-based Scholarships and Grants: List the number of degree-seeking full-time and less-then-full-time undergraduates who had no financial need and who were awarded institutional non-need-based scholarship or grant aid.
- Numbers should reflect the cohort awarded the dollars reported in H1.
- In the chart below, students may be counted in more then one row.

		First-time Full-time Freshmen	Full-time Undergrad (Incl-Fresh.)	Less Than Full-time Undergrad
N	Number of students in line **a** who had no financial need and who were awarded institutional non-need-based scholarship or grant aid (exclude those who were awarded athletic awards and tuition benefits)	241	1568	68
O	Average dollar amount of institutional non-need-based scholarship and grant aid awarded to students in line n	$ 6,180	$ 5,104	$ 3,823
P	Number of students in line **a** who were awarded an institutional non-need-based athletic scholarship pr grant	0	0	0
Q	Average dollar amount of institutional non-need-based athletic scholarships and grants awarded to students in line p			

This chart tells us that, at this particular school, there were 241 students in this freshman class who had no financial need and yet were awarded merit money. The average merit aid award for those students was $6,180. From Row P, we learn that no students at this college received athletic scholarships.

That's nice for the 241 students who received merit money, but that's 241 out of how many students? For that, you need to scroll up a bit in the Common Data Set to the chart in section H2 and look in Row A:

H2 **Number of Enrolled Students Awarded Aid:** List the number of degree-seeking full-time and less-than-full-time undergraduates who applied for and were awarded financial aid from any source.

- Aid that is non-need-based but that was used to meet need should be counted as **need-based aid.**
- Numbers should reflect the cohort awarded the dollars reported in H1.
- In the chart below, students may be counted in more than one row, and full-time freshmen should also be counted as full-time undergraduates.

		First-time Full-time Freshmen	Full-time Undergrad (Incl.Fresh)	Less Than Full-time Undergrad
A	Number of degree-seeking undergraduate students (CDS Item B1 if reporting on Fall 2020 cohort)	5739	25696	917
B	Number of students in line a who applied for need-based financial aid	3603	15564	461
C	Number of students in line b who were determined to have financial need	2677	11995	322
D	Number of students in line c who were awarded any financial aid	2526	11374	270
E	Number of students in line d who were awarded any need-based scholarship or grant aid	2514	11287	248
F	Number of students in line d who were awarded any need-based self-help aid	1932	8391	151
G	Number of students in line d who were awarded any non-need-based scholarship or grant aid	160	684	13
H	Number of students in line d whose need was fully met (exclude PLUS loans. unsubsidized loans, and private alternative loans)	309	1244	15
I	On average, the percentage of need that was met of students who were awarded any need-based aid. Exclude any aid that was awarded in excess of need as well as any resources that were awarded to replace EFC (PLUS loans, unsubsidized loans, and private alternative loans)	66.9%	62.2%	34.5%
J	The average financial aid package of those in line d. Exclude any resources that were awarded to replace EFC (PLUS loans, unsubsidized loans, and private alternative loans)	$ 41,094	$ 37,578	$ 14,351

We can see that there were 5,739 total students in this freshman class. Using simple division (241 out of 5,739), we get 0.042. So, 4.2% of the students received merit money. That's a very small percentage of students, and the average merit award is pretty meager as well. If your family is counting on merit aid rather than need-based aid to help pay for college, you might want to consider taking this college off your list.

If you do have financial need, this school is still not very helpful. Read the rows in chart H2. They tell us that 2,677 of the 5,739 total students (47%) were determined to have need. Of those, 2,514 were awarded need-based scholarships and grants (that is, free money). But only 309 students out of those 2,677 who had need had their need fully met. On average, this school only meets 66.9% of the need. That means that a student will get some money, but not all they really need to pay for this college. Their family would likely need to take out the balance in loans. The average financial aid package awarded was $41,094, while this college's Cost of Attendance is about $77,000.

The takeaway? A college like this one would be a good choice for families that are not cost conscious; it is not such a good choice, financially, for families with need, or for families with low need but who want merit aid.

Let's contrast that with one of the schools that is known for generosity for need-based aid, Dartmouth College. According to their Common Data Set, they had 1,221 freshmen in 2021, and 578 of those freshmen were determined to have financial need. On average, Dartmouth meets 100% of need for students enrolling. So, of those 578 students who were determined to have need, 564 were awarded scholarships or grants to the tune of about $60,000 each, plus loans of about $3,400 per student for that year. However, as is standard for the eight colleges of the Ivy League, Dartmouth does not offer any merit money.

WHERE SHOULD YOUR FAMILY START?

Now that you understand some of the fundamentals of college financial aid, start by determining your general income category relative to college costs: are you high income, low income, or somewhere in the middle? Here, the definition of high-, middle-, and low-income is solely based on how that income is viewed by the colleges. It's not related to, say, the federal poverty line. Your strategy for how you look at college costs will be based on your answer to that question.

HIGH-INCOME FAMILIES

High-income families are those that can pay the entire cost of attendance at a private college ($60,000+) each year without any significant impact on their day-to-day finances. These families usually have income of $300,000 or more per year from working or investments and correspondingly high assets. Their EFC is higher than the cost of most colleges, so they won't qualify for need-based aid.

While these families typically have no demonstrated need for financial assistance, they are likely to have some colleges offer them merit-based aid to entice the student to enroll at their institution. They do this because the colleges need to make sure to fill each incoming class. Not filling a class means lost revenue for each of the four years a student would have attended the school, so it's worth it to the colleges to discount a bit to ensure they are fully enrolled. In other words, yes, the colleges will offer money—sometimes quite significant money—to families that don't need it at all. I've had several students whose families were in the $250,000-or-more-per-year income category be offered merit scholarships of $100,000 ($25,000 per year for four years) at colleges on their lists.

These families can afford to let their student apply to whichever schools they like, since they are fine with paying full price if that's what it comes to. And while it's nice to have the merit money offered, it doesn't necessarily sway the outcome for these families. One of my students who earned a $100,000 merit scholarship at one college turned it down, deciding instead to attend USC (the University of Southern California) and pay full price rather than attend the school that offered the merit money.

LOW-INCOME FAMILIES

Again, "low-income" here is a matter of context. A family of four earning $85,000 or less would likely have a low SAI. The lower your SAI (EFC), the more need-based aid you should qualify for.

If your student is a high achiever (high GPA and/or test scores, strong extracurriculars, and demonstrated leadership), you should look for colleges that meet 100% of need, preferably with few or no loans. These colleges can be extremely selective, but very generous if your student can get admitted. For example, Stanford University states that undergraduate families with less than $75,000 per year in income will not be expected to pay tuition, room, or board. That said, even highly qualified students are regularly denied admission, so the student should not apply *only* to very selective schools.

These families should try to stay away from colleges that meet a lower percentage of need or that offer a lot of loans in their financial aid packages. That information is available in the Common Data Set, sections H2 and H5.

MIDDLE-INCOME FAMILIES

Most families I work with fall into this category, which gets squeezed from both ends. They make good money, so they don't qualify for much need-based aid, but they also can't just write a check for $85,000 per year for four years without flinching. Run your numbers. If you find that colleges are simply not affordable (that is, they do not offer an adequate amount of need-based or merit aid for your family), take them off the list *before* your student applies. Yes, this includes the Ivy League "dream" colleges and many others that simply don't offer merit scholarships. Focus instead on colleges that offer strong potential for merit scholarships where the student would be near the top of the incoming class in terms of their grades and/or test scores. This also means encouraging your student to hit the books and try to get the highest GPA possible, which can translate into scholarship money to help pay for college.

The other financial safety option for middle-income families is to apply to in-state universities to get the benefit of their state-tax-subsidized tuition (but this may have some downsides, as I'll discuss later when talking about four-year graduation rates). The third option, purely from an affordability perspective, is for the student to attend two years of community college and then transfer to a four-year school to finish their degree.

THE FINANCIAL AID AWARD LETTER

If the student is offered admission and your family has applied for financial aid, the school will send a financial aid award letter with the details of what the college is offering your student. Here's how a financial aid award letter from a public university broke down for one of my students who entered college as a freshman in 2019.

Costs in the 2019-2020 year	
Estimated Cost of Attendance	**$36,522/yr**
Tuition and fees	$ 14,184
Housing and meals	19,134
Books and supplies	870
Transportation	400
Other educational costs	1,934

Grants, Scholarships and Fee Waivers	
Total Grants, Scholarships and Fee Waivers	**$2,500/yr**
Grants and scholarships	$2,500
Federal Pell Grant	0
Grants from your state	0
Other scholarships you can use	0

What will you pay for college	
Net Cost	**$34,022/yr**
(Cost of attendance minus total grants and scholarships)	

Options to pay net costs

Work options	
Work-Study (Federal, state,or institutional)	$ 0

Student Loan Options (must be repaid)	
Federal Perkins Loans	$ 0
Federal Direct Subsidized Loan	0
Federal Direct Unsubsidized Loan	5,500

This student got $2,500 of "free" money (a grant or scholarship). That didn't do much to help offset the $36,522 cost of attendance. The college still expected this student and his mom—widowed but highly educated and well-employed—to contribute $34,022 per year. The letter included the option for the student to take out a Federal Direct Unsubsidized Loan for $5,500 to help cover the $34,022 net cost.

The maximum that students can currently borrow under this federal program is $5,500 in their freshman year, $6,500 in their sophomore year, $7,500 in their junior year, and another $7,500 in their senior year. Those are the *student* loans.

Parents can then borrow 100% of the difference using the federal PLUS (Parent Loan for Undergraduate Students) program. So, in this example, the student's mother could borrow $28,522 (that is, the $34,022 net cost minus the $5,500 student loan) via a PLUS loan.

Interest rates on these loans are fixed and change every July 1 for disbursements in the fall. This means that each year the student borrows money, the loans could have a different interest rate. Also, if parents make less than $180,000, they can deduct the interest they've paid on the Parent PLUS loan on their taxes.

Parents and students don't need to start paying back these loans until six months after the student graduates, although many families go ahead and pay the interest on those loans each year so that the interest does not compound.

Interestingly, these loans cannot be erased by a bankruptcy or transferred to another person (so, a parent cannot transfer the parent loan to the student after the student graduates). However, the student loan and the parent PLUS loan will be forgiven if (sorry to be morbid here) the student passes away, and the parent PLUS loan will be forgiven if the parent passes away. I've heard of at least one family with an elderly parent (the student's father was in his 80s) that put all the parent loans under that older parent's name, and when the father died a year or so after the student graduated from college, some $300,000 in accumulated college debt was forgiven.

Because of the delayed start of payments and forgiveness in the case of death, families should think carefully about whether to turn down these loans in favor of, say, taking a second mortgage on their home (instead of taking the loan), even if that mortgage repayment is at a lower interest rate than the federal parent loan.

In the case of the financial award letter example above, the college didn't offer the student a lot of help in paying for their education, but at least the college made it clear what was contained in each category. Some financial aid award letters can be much harder to decipher.

GO IN WITH EYES WIDE OPEN

Now that you know the fundamentals of how financial aid works, please take the time to sit down with your student (and your spouse, if applicable) and have a frank discussion about what your family is planning to contribute (which may or may not align with the EFC/SAI), what the student will be expected to pitch in, and which colleges should or should not be on the list based on the financial aid outlook for your student at each school. Review the student's list of 25 to 40 colleges and cull any for which the financial aid picture looks grim for your family. This will probably trim the list down to 20 to 25 colleges or so.

If you would like me to walk you through these financial aid concepts via video to help solidify your understanding, my online course, "Financial Aid: Key Concepts That Can Save You Thousands" is available at https://collegeprepcounseling. vipmembervault.com/.

There's nothing more heartbreaking than having a student earn admission to their top choice college, only to have to turn down the offer after determining that the college is just not financially feasible for the family. I'm delighted to know that you now have the tools to avoid that situation.

KEY TAKEAWAYS

1) Don't rule out a college based solely on its sticker price.
2) Don't use wishful thinking to say, "We'll find a way to pay" when there really is no good plan in place.
3) Almost every family should fill out the financial aid forms.
4) Take the time to crunch the numbers for each college on your student's list. This includes calculating your family's SAI and understanding how that will impact the financial aid you'll be offered from each college.
5) Understand the difference between need-based aid and merit-based aid.
6) Know which schools offer zero merit aid, and if your family or student will need merit aid to make a college affordable, make the decision early to cross no-merit-aid schools off the list.
7) Know which colleges require the CSS Financial Aid Profile® and how that will impact your family if you and the student's other parent are no longer married.
8) Know how to find, download, and search through the Common Data Set for each college on your student's list.
9) Be smart about how you borrow money to pay for college costs.

3

Building and Balancing
the Final List

You're making progress! You've narrowed the list of schools based on your student's criteria, and you have a picture of how each of those colleges will impact your family financially. You've removed any that don't make financial sense.

Now it's time to deeply research each college that remains on the list and trim it one final time to settle on a balanced list of 10 to 16 colleges to which your student will actually apply. This is the time to help your student discuss the details that would really draw them to each of those schools.

Your goal is to come up with that list of colleges that your student would love to attend, that will maximize the chances for your student to have several offers of admission by spring of senior year, and that make financial sense for your student and your family.

HOW TO RESEARCH COLLEGES

What do I mean by research in this context? At this stage, students should plan to spend about 30 minutes exploring the website for each college left on the list.

The first critical consideration when researching the school's website: have your student visit the Admissions section and confirm that they meet the minimum requirements for applicants to the overall college and the specific program or major to which they are applying.

For example, a college may require that applicants have three years of a foreign language (and yes, in most instances, starting a language in middle school will count toward one of those years). But if your student only has two years of foreign language, then there's a mismatch and the student's application may not even be read.

If you catch these kinds of issues early enough, there can be time to remedy any missing coursework in the summer after junior year or by adding a class in senior year. If not, and if a call to the admissions office confirms that the requirement is non-negotiable, then that college needs to come off the student's list. The student simply does not meet the criteria to be considered for admission. End of story and no wasted time spent writing essays or wasted money spent on application fees.

A few years ago, one of my California clients belatedly realized—in fall of his senior year—that he was missing the "one year of visual and performing arts" requirement for University of California (UC) admissions. He scrambled to arrange to take a class at the local community college that would squeeze a year's worth of content into one semester in spring of his senior year. It all worked out, and he's now at UC Berkeley, but at the time it added a layer of stress to the process.

In addition, some schools make their recommendations quite clear on their websites, without actually calling them requirements. For example, MIT wants to see that a student has taken physics, chemistry, biology, and math through calculus. While not a requirement per se, a student who hasn't taken those courses will not be as competitive in the application process at that hyper-selective school (with an admission rate of 4% for the Class of 2025).

For other competitive schools, the minimum requirements set the bar low for a student to apply, but those minimums are almost universally insufficient to earn an offer of admission. The applicant must show far more rigor and achievement than the minimum if they hope to be offered a spot. For example, at UCLA and UC Berkeley, an out-of-state student must have a minimum GPA of 3.4 to be eligible for admission, but it's extremely rare that a student with that GPA would be admitted unless there were special circumstances (such as being recruited for athletic talent). A more competitive weighted GPA for those schools, whether the student is in-state or out-of-state, would be in the 3.9–4.5+ range.

If your student has time to adjust their courses, or you have younger students moving through high school, it might be helpful to know this rule of thumb to prepare for selective college admissions: take four full years of each of the five core subjects. The student should plan to take four years each of English, history/social science, math, physical science (especially biology, chemistry, and physics), and four years of a single foreign language.

Next, the student should go into the "Academics" section of the college's website and hunt for the exact programs and classes they'd find interesting (they likely have this from the basic search they conducted to come up with their current college list) and professors they'd like to take classes from or under whom they'd like to try to do research.

While still on the college's website, the student should explore clubs and campus activities, the campus layout and buildings, and the school's traditions and rituals. I remember reading a "Why Johns Hopkins University?" essay a few years back in which a student was describing what events they would look forward to at JHU, and they mentioned "The Lighting of the Quads." I had no idea what that was, but quickly found videos of it on YouTube. It's a holiday tradition that brings the campus community together for a celebration right before winter finals and winter break. Simply by mentioning something unique to Johns Hopkins, this student demonstrated that they had researched the campus and envisioned what their life might be like if they were admitted. Another of my clients, a future mechanical engineer and drone enthusiast, was delighted to discover the Ford Robotics Building and M-Air outdoor drone testing lab at the University of Michigan. Those are the kinds of details your student should be looking for when exploring campuses online.

As the parent, you can help by digging up each college's four-year graduation rate, as I mentioned back in Chapter 1. You want your student to be able to graduate in four years and know that that's the norm at each college to which they apply. It will skyrocket the cost of their education if it takes them five or six years to get the classes they need (or if they change their major too many times and end up taking longer). It may demotivate them if too many of their classmates drop out before finishing. You and your student need to know what percentage of the students who start at that college stick around for four years and are able to complete their degree in that time frame.

Next up: visit the college's official channel on YouTube and watch any videos that look interesting or enlightening. If the student likes what they see at this point, ask the student to keep digging a little further afield, away from the college's marketing-department-approved messages. What do the school's students say on YouTube, Reddit, or the online community at College-Confidential.com? What are some of the reviews and comments about the college on Niche.com?

After all that research, is the student more interested in the college or less? Where does it fall on their priority list compared to the other colleges … and why? Being able to articulate what they love about a college is critical to their decision regarding whether to (and why they would) apply.

THE 4X PAYOFF OF TAKING DETAILED NOTES

Researching colleges takes time, something often in short supply for high school juniors. I'm all about efficiency. I don't want students to spend time doing research at this juncture and then have to go do it again at different stages later in the process. So, I'll tell you right now that they should take careful, detailed digital notes—including copying and pasting the URLs to key pages on a college's website—during this initial research phase. They can then use that research at four different stages in this process.

First, as I mentioned, they'll use their research to determine if they even want to apply to a particular college. Detailed notes will help them remember, weeks or months from now, why they did or did not include that college on their final list.

Second, if they decide to apply to a college that asks the "Why Our College?" essay question, they'll use that research to help them write a very detailed and specific answer (see Chapter 11).

Third, they'll revisit those notes before heading into a college interview with an admissions representative or alum from that college to remind them of talking points they'll want to mention (see Chapter 15).

And fourth, in spring of senior year, when they must select among a handful of offers from different colleges, they'll go to their notes one last time to help them decide where they'll actually enroll, and they'll clearly be able to articulate why they've chosen that college (see Chapter 17).

BALANCING THE LIST AMONG LIKELY, TARGET, REACH, AND LOTTERY SCHOOLS

As a final step in building the list, you and the student should sort the remaining colleges by the student's chances of getting admitted based on their academic track record and (if available) test scores. Those are two of the key components (but not the only components) that will help determine the student's likelihood of admission to each school on their list. The goal is to make sure they have a balanced list of likely, target, and, optionally, reach and "lottery" schools.

Likely schools are those where your student is extremely likely to be offered admission. As a rule of thumb, these schools accept more than 70% of the students who apply.

Target schools are those where the student has about a 50–50 chance of being admitted. The student's credentials (GPA, test scores, leadership, extracurriculars) align with those of most students who are admitted, but the school simply can't accept all the qualified students who apply. These schools often accept 35%–70% of applicants.

Reach schools are those for which the student's credentials fall short compared to those of most students who are admitted (for example, the GPA or extracurriculars are a bit low) or there are, again, simply many more qualified students than the college can admit. Reach schools only accept 20%–35% of students who apply.

Lottery schools are those that have admission rates below 20%. They regularly turn down amazing students who are perfectly well qualified, resulting in admission becoming almost like winning a lottery.

The final list should be made up entirely of colleges that your student would be happy to attend, and it should have enough likely and target schools that they will almost certainly have offers of admission after all the decisions come back in the spring.

A balanced list might have four likely, four target, four reach, and two lottery schools. A balanced list could even have no lottery or reach schools at all, in which case the student could apply to fewer schools overall, so perhaps four target and four likely schools.

Problems arise when the student's list is not balanced. Those lists are too heavy on reach and lottery schools (for example, one likely, one target, four reach, and six lottery schools). An unbalanced list might leave the student with few or even no offers of admission come spring of senior year.

Keep in mind that one student's reach school may be another student's likely school. A student with a 4.5 GPA and outstanding extracurriculars will have a different set of target and likely schools than a student with a 3.3 GPA and no extracurriculars.

We had a student here in my town a few years ago who was not a client, but I was Facebook friends with his mom. When her son hit senior year and college application time, the mom thought they had everything well in hand. As I discovered later, her son had a 4.2 GPA and solid test scores. He was not applying to the Ivy League, so she figured—and the whole family thought, apparently—that they had this college admissions thing down, no problem. Then, in the spring, she uploaded this heartbreaking post: "Please hold a good thought for my brilliant, funny, kind, and wonderful teen, who has had some disappointing college news."

This student was not admitted to a single one of the eight colleges he applied to, which is terribly discouraging, especially in light of his 4.2 GPA (that result made me wish I had offered them some help, but it had seemed at the outset like they had everything under control). I ended up talking to the mom later to deconstruct what had happened. In essence, they miscalculated the difficulty of the admissions chances at the schools on his list that they thought were "likelies." The student basically got shut out because he didn't have a balanced list.

To keep things objective and take some of the emotion and opinion out of this process, I give my clients access to proprietary software that gathers information on the student's GPA, the rigor of their classes, their test scores, the depth of their extracurricular and volunteer involvement, their leadership, the likely strength of their letters of recommendation, and their talents. It aligns those qualifications with the colleges on the student's list, then churns out a custom summary of the student's admissions chances at those specific schools. The program sorts the colleges on the student's list into five easy-to-understand color categories. Purple is for the schools that will almost surely accept the student ("likelies"). Blue is for those that will probably accept them (also "likelies"). Green is for schools where the student has about a 50–50 chance of getting in ("targets"). Orange is for the schools where the student would have difficulty earning an offer of admission ("reaches"). And red is for the schools that are truly a long shot ("lottery").

If students run their list through the program and come out with ten schools in the red category and four in the orange category, we know the list is unbalanced and we trim the number of red schools and add schools in the other categories.

That software also tells us how the student compares in several categories (GPA, test scores, academic rigor, and extracurriculars) to students who are accepted at each college. If we see in early summer that the extracurriculars category is a little low compared to students who were admitted, we find ways to shore up the student's credentials in that category in the summer before the applications are due.

Although the software makes it easy, you can piece together this information on your own through—you guessed it!— the Common Data Set. Find section C, the information on First-Time, First-Year Admissions for students (those are the freshmen!). You'll see how many students applied, how many were admitted, and how many enrolled. Many schools will also report the percentage of admitted students who had an unweighted GPA of 4.0, the percentage of enrolled students whose GPA was between 3.75 and 4.0, the percentage whose GPA was between 3.50 and 3.74, etc. You can see how your student's GPA compares.

The Common Data Set will also list the percentage of enrolled students who submitted SAT® or ACT® assessment scores, and what the middle 50th percentile range is for those scores (so you can compare how your student's scores align).

Using the Common Data Set information, your student can determine whether their grades and test scores are above average for students enrolled at a school (making that school a likely), whether their grades and scores are on par with those of enrolled students (making that school a target), or whether their grades and scores are a bit below those of most enrolled students (making that school a reach or even a lottery). That is how you and your student can use the data provided in the Common Data Set to tease out whether a college is a likely, target, reach, or lottery school for their list.

It is certainly not required that a student have any lottery schools or even any reach schools on their list. Without those, they can trim the list of colleges down to about eight likely and target schools, saving them a lot of time and effort (and saving you a bunch of application fees) in the process.

If going through each college's Common Data Set seems overwhelming, you can follow a less precise guideline. Assuming your student has a reasonably strong GPA (3.5–3.8 range) and some solid extracurriculars, then you can assume that colleges with a 65% admission rate or higher are likely schools. A 35%–65% admission rate would be target schools. A 20%–35% admission rate would be reach schools. And less than a 20% admission rate would be lottery schools. Again, that general ballpark doesn't take into account the student's specifics, but it should at least give you an inkling that there's an imbalance if your student has only reach and lottery schools on the list. As a double check, have your student run their college list past their school counselor to confirm whether it is balanced.

My goal for my clients is to have their final college list set by mid-June after they finish their junior year. This allows us to gather those colleges' essay prompts or, more precisely, the essay prompts those colleges used the previous year, since the prompts don't tend to change a whole lot from year to year. That gives the student the opportunity to write as many of the required essays as possible over the summer, so they are well on their way to completing the applications before school starts in the fall.

KEY TAKEAWAYS

1) Know how to guide your student in searching for admissions prerequisites for each college on the list. If your student is missing any required classes, determine if there's a way the student can fit those in before the end of senior year.
2) Help your student learn to comb through a college's website to research the core curricular requirements, major requirements, classes, and faculty.
3) Parents can research the four-year graduation rates of the colleges on the list.
4) Understand how to balance the list. A good rule of thumb for a balanced list is to have four likely, four target, four reach, and two lottery schools.

4

Creating a Résumé

There are approximately 25,000 high school valedictorians in the United States each year. In 2019, an estimated 22,000 students earned perfect scores on their SAT®. For the class of 2025, Harvard received 57,786 applications and admitted 2,320. Stanford admits 1,700. My point in sharing this data is that even a student who is valedictorian of their school or has perfect test scores needs something else in their background to earn an offer of admission from the country's most selective schools. These schools will regularly deny admission to a student who has incredibly high grades and test scores if that student doesn't also have amazing extracurricular activities or outside interests. That means that the top students differentiate themselves from their peers through their activities inside and outside of school. They've found extracurriculars they love that also make an impact in their school or their communities, often on a state, regional, or national level. Even colleges that are not as selective want students who have been involved in their schools and communities and who will bring a positive attitude and a history of engagement with them onto campus.

Students tell the colleges about their extracurricular activities in two ways: a résumé and an activities list. They essentially tell the same information in two different formats, but I like to have students create the résumé first and then use that as a reference to create the activities list. We'll talk about the activities lists more when we discuss the application portals in Chapter 13.

RÉSUMÉ

For my clients, I've found that creating a résumé early in the college application process is helpful for several reasons.

First, it forces the student, with help from the parents, to remember and write down details about all the activities they have been involved with since they started 9th grade. Do not go as far back as middle school unless the student participated in a National Spelling Bee or another very significant award.

Second, it assists students in identifying patterns in how they've chosen to spend their time, enabling them to reflect on which extracurriculars they've loved and which, if any, might guide them toward a potential college major or career of interest and could certainly help them come up with ideas for application essays.

Third, creating a résumé gives the student a starting point for filling in their list of activities in the actual college applications (I'll cover that in the next section).

The résumé is helpful because it can offer those reading applications with details and information that won't fit on the activities list, which severely limits how much the student can write. I mean that literally. The Common App form allows only 150 characters—letters and spaces—to describe activities. Colleges want to admit students who will be active and engaged on campus, and they assume that students who were involved in extracurricular activities in high school are the same students who will bring energy, enthusiasm, and passion to their college community. They're looking for evidence of that in the résumé and activities list.

The best practice, if the student wants to ensure proper formatting of the final résumé within the college application itself, is to save it as a PDF file before uploading it to the application portal. Also, have the student name the file appropriately (such as, "Samantha Khan Resume.pdf") rather than something generic ("Resume.pdf").

Students can create a basic black-and-white, text-only résumé (in Microsoft Word or in a Google Doc), or they can opt for a more graphic résumé using one of the free templates available on websites such as Canva.com.

The résumé templates on Canva.com are generally set up for people entering the workforce and so will have "Work Experience" listed first, whereas students still in high school should have "Education" as the first section.

There is no set-in-stone format for a résumé to follow. Generally, grouping the core information in an easy-to-read way is the key. All student résumés should start with the student's name and contact information and information about their school and education:

- Student's name, email, and phone. It may or may not include their home address.
- Education: school name, city, state, GPA, and expected date of graduation, plus any information that may be relevant (IB® diploma candidate, honors society, etc.)

Additional categories for an academic résumé might (but do not have to) include:

- Honors and Awards
- Volunteer or Community Service Experiences
- Athletics
- Arts
- Interests and Hobbies
- Paid Work
- Skills

Entries should be organized by category, but the categories will vary based on the student's activities. One student may have a category of "Government and Politics" if they've been politically active. Another might have a "Social Justice" section or a "Technology" section.

I recommend to my clients that they start by informally listing all their activities and then grouping the activities together in a way that makes sense. The categories then become clear based on the groupings.

Often, each individual listing within a résumé will start with the position the student held, then the name and location of the organization (city and state), the hours per week spent, and the time frame in which the student participated (9th grade, 10th grade, etc.), then a quick description of what the student did in the role and any data on impacts or outcomes (how many people served, how many games won, etc.). For example:

Captain, Summerville High School Varsity Lacrosse, Summerville, PA

8 hours/week, 12 weeks/year, 9th-12th grades

Voted to captain role by teammates and the coach. Organized team meetings; assisted coach in developing the training schedule; helped resolve team conflicts, boosted the morale of the team members. Won 16 of 20 games against 10 rival teams; took the team to the state championships.

Since most students have never written a résumé and don't know how to summarize or highlight the most important facets of their accomplishments, it's a good idea to encourage them to accept your help and guidance or the guidance of another adult who has experience with résumé-style writing.

Unless a student is going to actually use this résumé to search for a summer job or internship, they can go ahead and fill it in with a forward-looking lens. The résumé will be uploaded to the application portals in fall of senior year, so the student might as well write in "high school senior, expected graduation June of 2023" or "Volleyball Team, 9th, 10th, 11th, 12th" rather than using their current status as a junior and ending it with 11th grade (assuming they know what their activities will be senior year). It's not imperative to do that, but it helps decrease the updates that would need to be made in the fall.

KEY TAKEAWAYS

1) The résumé and activities list are critical components of your student's application. They help the colleges understand how your student has chosen to spend their time and what's important to them.

2) Help your student keep a list of activities from the beginning of 9th grade.

3) Help them understand what résumé format looks like and sounds like.

5

Articulating the Student's Story

A student who can clearly and persuasively articulate who they are and what they seek in their college experience will have an advantage in the admissions process. Keep in mind that admissions officers are tasked with reviewing hundreds or even thousands of applications during an application cycle, which means they take only a few minutes to review a single application (yes, it's that short—those who are tasked with reviewing 60 applications per day in a ten-hour day get 10 minutes per application, or only 7.5 minutes per application if they're trying to work an eight-hour day).

With that kind of time crunch, it's simply easier for the application reader's brain to absorb, categorize, and make a positive decision if the information they are reading about the applicant all fits together in a way that makes sense.

When I'm describing the importance of clear messaging to my clients over Zoom, I hold up two Rubik's Cubes. The first one is solved; the six faces of the cube correctly show nine small squares of each of the colors—red, blue, green, orange, yellow, and white. The second cube is a jumble, showing the colors all mixed up with no rhyme or reason. I want my students to create an application that presents the different sides of their personality in such a way that, like the solved Rubik's Cube, everything fits together and makes sense even with only a quick glance.

Knowing this, and simply to make a more compelling argument as to why they should be admitted, the student should think about the entire application they plan to submit and make sure that the different parts and pieces work in harmony. Their application package—grades, test scores, extracurriculars, recommendations, and essays—will have more impact on the reader if the student can identify clear story threads or patterns to highlight in their application.

Here's an example of what not to do. A student may tell a college that they are interested in studying biology and eventually applying to medical school. But if they didn't take biology in high school, or received a poor grade in that class, or their only essay discusses how much they love art, it's going to leave the application reader confused.

Here's a better approach. One of my students was interested in a career in medicine, either as a pharmacist or a physician. She had aligned all the faces of her proverbial Rubik's Cube: she had taken rigorous math and science courses in high school, including AP® Biology, and had earned top grades in those classes. During the COVID-19 pandemic, she volunteered at a local clinic to monitor newly vaccinated people for side effects during the 15-minute post-shot waiting period. She had done a summer internship at a medical lab in her town to learn about DNA sequencing and had shadowed a pharmacist during his shift at an emergency room, getting a behind-the-scenes glimpse of the organized chaos surrounding emergency treatment of a patient. She not only used these experiences to confirm and deepen her commitment to a career in medicine, but these experiences gave her great stories and anecdotes to share in her essays.

In addition, she wasn't one-dimensional. As a member of her school's cross-country team, she was able to write an essay about her running team that complemented her academic and career interests. Those stories showed her as a dedicated team player who was committed to her health. Overall, her class choices, extracurriculars, grade patterns, and essay topics all aligned in a way that made the whole of her application work well as a unit.

Contrast that to a student who says he wants to be a physician because he watched a grandparent suffer through cancer and would like to find a cure. But he hadn't taken a rigorous load of science courses, nor taken the initiative to seek internships or opportunities to find out what that career path entails day-to-day. On top of that, in the early drafts of his essays, he focused on his love of basketball. There was no tie-in to his academic interests at all, so his application didn't work together as a cohesive whole.

For this student, we went back to square one to rethink how he wanted to present himself in his college applications because there wasn't enough evidence from his background to shore up his claim to be interested in medicine. We needed to look for another angle or approach that was more strongly supported by his actual activities. We found a way to shift his focus slightly, to athletic training and physical therapy. He started volunteering that spring as a trainer with the track and field team, added an anatomy and physiology class to his senior year schedule, and was able to write about athletics, movement, and injuries in his essays. Rubik's Cube solved.

--------------------- **Pro Tip** ---------------------

Pre-med is not a major. A student can major in art or history or Russian literature in college and still apply to medical school, as long as they take the prerequisite courses (organic chemistry, biology, etc.). They'll need a strong GPA and relevant extracurriculars, but the major per se is not the key factor.

Here's another example. For a student interested in studying history, it would make sense to have taken honors or advanced classes in U.S., European, or world history (or a combination of those), volunteered at a museum or historical society if that opportunity was available in the local area, and pursued summer opportunities focused on history, etc. Of course, an essay that helps the reader understand how the student's passion for history developed is like a little bow on top of a gift. It ties the whole thing together.

Here's another aspect of the application narrative. Let's say a student is applying to college and declaring that they are interested in eventually pursuing a law degree. The student has participated on the Mock Trial team, completed an internship in a judge's or lawyer's office over the summers, and taken courses that would enhance their ability to write clearly and develop their skills in analysis, critical thinking, and research. The essays detail the student's experiences and what they've learned about the field and about themselves. The work that the student has already done makes it easier for the admissions reader to see that the student has tested the waters and knows, *based on experiences,* that this career is a good fit.

As a parent, you can support your student by discussing their goals, dreams, and the theme of their application, even casually over dinner or on a car ride. Planting seeds of ideas for them to consider, especially early in the process (that is, the middle of the junior year) can pay off once they sit down to work on their applications.

Sometimes, simply the time spent going through the college application process and digging into the courses that colleges offer for each specific major helps the student uncover an interest they might not have been able to articulate before. One of my students came into the process looking for colleges that offered a major in astronomy, but, as she looked around the various colleges' websites and academic offerings, she realized that the courses that comprised environmental science fit with her interests even better—and happened to align with the extracurricular activities she'd been doing all along. She, in effect, changed her proposed major during the application process—which is just fine! This is very much a time when the students are learning to define themselves, and this may be the first time they've been asked to do some self-reflection and deeper thinking on the direction they'd like their lives to take.

With my clients, I find that the student's résumé is the first place to look when thinking through what might become the student's organizing theme (if it's not already obvious).

What activities and subjects really light up the student? What have they been drawn to since they were small? That is something that you, as the parent, can help them see. I'm reminded of the background story of Japanese organizer Marie Kondo of the KonMari Method. When she was in second grade, she apparently preferred to spend her recess time indoors, organizing the classroom bookshelves. All these years later, she's been able to leverage that early interest in keeping things neat and organized into a publishing and speaking empire. So, help the student identify habits and interests that they've been naturally drawn to all their lives. It might help in this process.

Pro Tip

At most schools, students can indicate an interest in a particular major in their applications but then change their minds after they land on campus and discover interests in subjects they may not have been exposed to in high school. That said, for certain majors, especially engineering, computer science, business, nursing, and film studies, it can be very difficult for a student to transfer into those later on, so students would be wise to check the policies at the schools they are interested in. If they truly want to pursue one of those majors, they should apply directly to that major in their applications.

What about a student who is undecided? I do think it makes it easier on the admissions officers if a student has a direction that aligns the different parts of their application, but if a student is simply interested in many things, then be authentic in the application and say so. In that case, it's better to describe specific interests across subjects ("I love history for the way it illuminates how our current political world came to be, but I also love math and geometry for their elegant symmetry") rather than default to a vague sense of purposelessness ("I have no idea what I want to study").

Articulating the student's interests not only helps clarify the application as a whole, but it is key to figuring out which colleges should be on the student's list, as we noted in Chapter 1 when we discussed the college search. This is not always easy, but it's critical work to help students determine the best choice for the path forward at this point (note: I am *not* saying they should be deciding what they want to do for the rest of their lives—we're only looking a few steps ahead).

If the student needs to write multiple essays for a single college, they should think of the essays like the different sides of the Rubik's Cube. Each essay should bring in a different color or aspect of who they are and how they came to develop their values, interests, etc. They don't all have to tie back to the main theme, but the essays should work together in terms of the application as a whole.

KEY TAKEAWAYS

1) Your student's college application will likely be read in under ten minutes, so they need a clear narrative that the reader can understand quickly.
2) The application components—grades, test scores, extra-curriculars, recommendations, and essays—need to work in concert to help the reader see where the student came from and where they are headed.
3) Look to the student's activities list to identify a theme or pattern for the application if one isn't already apparent.

6

Testing

Before COVID, standardized tests such as the ACT® and SAT® were a rite of passage that most students had to slog through if they wanted to apply to a majority of the selective schools in the United States. But the restrictions of the pandemic meant that many students weren't able to test, so almost all the colleges switched their application requirements to make testing optional. Each individual student, then, must now decide whether or not to test, and that is a decision that you as a parent can help them think through.

During COVID, students who managed to take an SAT® or ACT® exam and felt they earned a strong score could submit those scores to the colleges to shore up their applications. If students couldn't take an exam, or took an exam and did not score well, they could still apply under the "test optional" policies at many colleges.

As it turned out, those SAT® and ACT® exams were keeping a lot of students from applying to the most selective colleges, and, once that barrier came down, applications skyrocketed in fall of 2020. Colgate University in Hamilton, New York, saw a 102.6% increase in applications that fall—more than double the number they had received a year earlier. Harvard applications went up 43% and MIT applications went up 65%. According to a report in *Forbes* magazine, the increase in applications came largely from minority and low-income students, giving the selective colleges an opportunity to increase their diversity on campus.

Nevertheless, it seems as though many colleges still like the reassurance of a strong test score. During a recent post-COVID admission cycle, chatter among admissions counselors indicated that Auburn University in Alabama, which purported to be test optional, seemed to be turning down a significant number of strong candidates who did not submit test scores in favor of academically weaker candidates (as measured by their grade point average) who did submit test scores. In addition, MIT announced in the spring of 2022 that they were reinstating the test score requirement as part of their application.

Another consequence of colleges going test-optional is that the average scores are going up because students with lower scores are simply choosing not to send those scores to colleges. If the lower scores aren't being submitted, and only the higher scores are being sent, then the average of the submitted scores goes up.

In general, for students applying to the most selective colleges, it can be an advantage to have high test scores versus no test scores at all. Low test scores, on the other hand, can be a detriment. I recommend that you work with your student to research the score range for each college on their list, and then determine how close your student is to hitting the 50th percentile or higher. If they can hit that, submit the scores. If not, perhaps refrain from submitting the scores, but be aware that some colleges that claim to be test optional seem to heavily favor those students who do submit scores.

How do you find those percentiles? My team has already gathered for you the SAT® and ACT® statistics for the most popular 200 or so colleges in the U.S.; you can access that spreadsheet through this book's resources page at https://www. CollegePrepCounseling.com/resources. Or you can gather the information yourself by going back to the Common Data Set, this time to section C9. Here's an example of what the information will tell you for the reporting school:

Percent of first-time, first-year (freshman) students with scores in each range:

Score Range	SAT Evidence-Based Reading and Writing	SAT Math
700-800	59.74%	62.39%
600-699	32.30%	28.76%
500-599	7.52%	8.85%
400-499	0.44%	0.00%
300-399	0.00%	0.00%
200-299	0.00%	0.00%
Totals should = 100%	100.00%	100.00%

Score Range	SAT Composite
1400-1600	62.84%
1200-1399	30.97%
1000-1199	6.19%
800-999	0.00%
600-799	0.00%
400-599	0.00%
Totals should = 100%	100.00%

Score Range	ACT Composite	ACT English	ACT Math
30-36	77.05%	81.64%	58.59%
24-29	19.84%	13.67%	35.55%
18-23	3.11%	4.69%	5.86%
12-17	0.00%	0.00%	0.00%
6-11	0.00%	0.00%	0.00%
Below 6	0.00%	0.00%	0.00%
Totals should = 100%	100.00%	100.00%	100.00%

If you have a student who has extreme test anxiety or simply doesn't do well in standardized testing, you may be able to relieve some of the pressure on the student (and save money on test prep) by skipping the tests altogether. Instead, they can spend that saved time increasing their involvement in interesting activities. That would be a mental-health and life win for the student. But yes, having a fabulous test score will help their application.

TEST BLIND

While many colleges consider test scores as part of your application if you choose to submit them, other schools—notably the schools in the University of California and California State University systems—are now test blind. Even if your student has perfect ACT® or SAT® scores, those scores will not be considered in their application, hence the term "test blind." (Note: students can still submit their scores to fulfill minimum eligibility requirements or for course placement once the student is on campus, but the scores are not considered for admission.)

If you have a student who is interested in testing, here are a few guidelines that may be helpful.

HAVE THE STUDENT SET UP A FOR-COLLEGE-ONLY EMAIL

Before the student ever signs up with the College Board® (for the PSAT/NMSQT® and SAT® tests) or ACT, Inc. (for the ACT® assessment), I recommend that they create a new email account to use solely for the college admissions process. Once the testing organizations get hold of the student's email address and other personal information, the student will often be inundated with email and brochures from colleges.

Parents often want to know how they can help their student in this process without overstepping. One way you can help is to get your child's permission to access their for-colleges-only email address to help them manage the incoming flood of correspondence. With the student's permission, you could unsubscribe from or block colleges that are not on the student's potential interest list. You can open and read the emails from colleges that are of interest (and click on the links inside the emails, as the colleges track that!). And you can keep the student informed of those emails that are most important and that they should read themselves.

Keeping the college emails separate from their personal emails will also keep the personal email account from being flooded by college information, which can add to the stress students sometimes feel around this process.

PSAT/NMSQT®

The Preliminary SAT/National Merit Scholarship Qualifying Test® is offered in October and is usually taken by juniors and some sophomores. About 3% of top-scoring students who take the exam as juniors qualify for recognition in the National Merit Scholarship program. Students can be recognized as Commended, Semi-Finalists, or Finalists. This is an academic honor that the student can list in their applications and that will be noticed by the colleges. If your school doesn't already require students to take this test, then make sure your student registers through their school in early September. The PSAT/NMSQT®

score can also be used to estimate how well the student might do on the SAT® exam.

SAT® AND ACT®

Students who want to send standardized test scores to the colleges on their list can pick which of the two main assessments—the SAT® or the ACT®—they'd like to take. They do not have to take both! It really is a matter of preference, and it is worth spending a weekend to take a proctored practice exam for each of these to determine which one best suits the student. Many test prep companies will offer this to students for a minimal charge. It's important that the two tests be taken close together so that other factors (such as new material learned in school) will not skew the results. The student can then compare their scores across the two tests to see if they naturally tend to do better on one of those formats. If so, that's the test the student should prep for.

TIMING OF THE TESTS

I advise students to plan to take their first test in spring of junior year (January or March), and then retake in May or June if they want to try to nudge their scores up with a second sitting. Some colleges will take a "superscore" which collects the student's highest score in each section from any test administration, giving the student a higher overall score than they earned in any single sitting. Only if the student is determined to make a third go of it do I recommend testing in August or in September of their senior year. It's best to get all the testing done before senior year begins.

Scheduling the testing early also builds a cushion in case the tests are canceled for any reason. A lot of testing was canceled during COVID, but I've also had a student whose test was canceled because a California wildfire made the testing center uninhabitable on the day of the test (too much smoke). I've had students fall ill on the day of the test. And I had one student continually find excuses to put off registering for the test. He finally signed up for the last possible test date, in December of his senior year. He really needed a strong test to shore up his low GPA ... and then the testing center closed due to COVID. So don't let your student wait until the last minute to get their testing done.

SENDING OFFICIAL SCORES TO THE COLLEGES

Once a student has determined which colleges they'll be applying to, you as the parent can help by carefully reviewing each school's test policy. Are test scores optional, required, or not considered? If required, does the college want the student to self-report their scores in the application (to be verified at a later date) or do they want the student to send an official score report from the testing organization (ACT, Inc. or the College Board®). It can take those companies a long time to get the scores sent out (and it can cost money to have them sent as well), so placing the order early will save on fees to expedite the sending of the scores at the last minute.

Once my students are done testing, we review their scores against the middle 50% of the scores submitted by students who were admitted to each of their colleges. If their score falls in that top 50%, they submit. If the scores don't fall in that range, they do not submit (when they have that option). Most end up submitting scores to their likely and target schools, but only occasionally to their reach schools.

KEY TAKEAWAYS

1) Testing is still important. A great test score can help your student get an offer of admission.

2) Help your student decide if testing and test prep are likely to pay off for them. For students with extreme test anxiety or who generally do very poorly on standardized tests, skipping the tests altogether is a viable option.

3) As a parent, you can help with information gathering by finding the top 50th percentile scores for each college on the student's list so that it's easier to decide which schools should get the student's scores and which should not.

4) Have the student set up a for-colleges-only email account that you, as the parent, can access.

5) Make sure your student registers for and takes the PSAT/NMSQT® in October of their junior year.

6) Work with your student to map out when they'll be taking the tests and help them with the registration process.

7) Parents can be in charge of figuring out which colleges allow students to self-report their scores (for most private schools, this information is in the Common App) and which require that scores be sent from the testing agencies. Then you as the parent can arrange to send those scores (and pay the fee that goes along with that).

7

The Critical Role of the High School Counselor

Whether the student attends a public or a private high school, the school counselor will play a key role in supporting the student's college application. Your student will need the counselor's cooperation and timely attention to all the details. Without a positive recommendation from the counselor and their help turning in the school materials on time, the student's application may be relegated to the "deny" pile. For these reasons, it's important for your student to keep the counselor informed about which schools are on their list and the deadlines for those applications.

As the parent, you can encourage your student to make an extra effort to connect with the counselor early and often. Have the student make an appointment to go in for a discussion about what the student is looking for and the proposed college list. The vast majority of counselors really like to help, so give them the opportunity to share their knowledge.

Although the student completes the part of the application that includes their personal data and essays, the school counselor is responsible for coordinating and sending all the documentation required from the high school (including early transcripts, the school profile, the counselor's letter of recommendation, and final transcripts). Each college needs to receive both the student's portion and the counselor's supporting materials in order for the student's application to be considered complete.

Remember, too, that many high school counselors are swamped. Be gracious with them as they try to juggle all their responsibilities. As one school counselor posted to one of my online counseling groups (IEC stands for "independent educational consultant"—that's me!):

> "In my schools, very few, if any, students used outside IEC help. I know because of the counseling I need to do. [School] counselors don't generally work over the summer, so the September/October flood of essays, and sometimes very bad essays, that need immediate attention at the same time we're straightening out and issuing transcripts is a huge hurdle. Lists, in my experience, are never finalized the previous spring, so many show up in September with nary a clue, even though early prep is repeatedly mentioned as a best practice in countless meetings leading up to grade 12."

If possible, have your student show their counselor a preliminary college list in spring, help your student check their transcript for any errors before the end of junior year, and ensure there's time for the student to crank out their essays (with appropriate reviewers) over the summer.

SCHOOL PROFILE

The school profile is a document that the counselor sends to the colleges to provide information about the school and student body. How many students attend the school? How many students are on free and reduced-cost lunch? What percentage of students graduate, and how many go on to attend two- or four-year colleges? How many advanced courses are offered?

The school profile helps the colleges understand the context of the applicant's background. For example, if a student reports taking three Advanced Placement® courses out of only three that were offered, then that student pursued the most rigorous curriculum available at their school. If a student reports taking three Advanced Placement® courses out of 14 that were offered, that shows that the student did not pursue the most rigorous curriculum available.

A few years ago, I worked with a student from rural Michigan who attended a tiny private high school that did not offer any Advanced Placement® courses. She decided to drive across town to take two AP® classes at the local public high school, demonstrating to the colleges on her list that she was willing to go above and beyond in pursuit of more challenging academics. Even if she hadn't mentioned that specifically in her application anywhere, the colleges would have seen from the school profile that she didn't have those advanced course options available at her school.

You can find links to example school profiles here: https://www.CollegePrepCounseling.com/resources.

NAVIANCE AND SCOIR

Many high schools and their counseling teams use software to keep track of their students' college applications and paperwork. Two of the most popular are Naviance and SCOIR.

If your student's school uses one of these (or another third-party software program) to help manage their students' college applications, be sure that your student has the site's URL and knows their username and password. If the school counselor has invested time in setting up these tracking systems to help the students, and if the counselor uses the system to communicate key college-related information to students, then the student should spend time exploring the site, learning to navigate it, and discovering what tools it may have to help manage their applications. Parents are often given a login and password as well and can help support their student by familiarizing themselves with the platform.

TRANSCRIPTS

The school counselor is responsible for getting student transcripts to the schools on the student's list, so the student needs to keep the counselor informed about where they are planning to apply.

After the spring admission results are out and the student has made a commitment to attend one college, the student will also need to inform the counselor of their choice so the counselor can send the final high school transcript to that college after graduation. (Note: if grades slip in the second half of senior year, colleges can revoke their offers of admission.)

LIAISON WITH THE COLLEGES

College admissions representatives are often assigned to certain geographical areas of the country. They are the main point of contact between a high school and the college, and if a counselor has worked at a particular high school for a number of years, they sometimes have long-term business relationships with college representatives. This can help students resolve issues ranging from missing documentation to special circumstances that might arise. On occasion, a school counselor can go to bat for a student, putting in an extra phone call to pass along a good word for that student's application—another reason the student should make the effort to get to know their school counselor.

DON'T FORGET TO THANK THEM

If a school counselor has taken the time to write your student a letter of recommendation and helped manage the forms for their applications, it would be gracious of the student to drop off a thank-you note (not just an email, but a card or note on actual paper) after the applications are all submitted.

After May 1, it's appropriate to send a follow-up note informing the counselor where they were admitted and which college the student has decided to attend. The applications are a lot of work, and the fun part is hearing the results and knowing that the student is heading off to an exciting new adventure on a college campus. And, as I mentioned before, the counselor still has to send the student's final transcript to the college where the student plans to enroll.

KEY TAKEAWAYS

1) Encourage your student to get to know their counselor as early in their high school career as possible. Keep them informed about the activities (especially those outside of school) that the student participates in.

2) During the application season, make sure the counselor has an opportunity to weigh in on the college list, and that your student keeps the counselor informed about which colleges, specifically, the student is applying to and what deadlines they need to meet. This allows the counselor to send all the right documents to the right colleges at the appropriate time.

3) Find a copy of the school profile for your student's school so you know what information the colleges are receiving.

4) Learn whether your student's high school uses Naviance, SCOIR, or another system to track students' college admissions forms. Make sure your student knows how to log in to and use that system. If you can get a parent account or access, then you can help your student track their status.

5) Provide small notecards or stationery for your student to write thank-you notes to the teachers and counselor who wrote their recommendations.

8

Letters of Recommendation

In an attempt to get more insight into a student's abilities and character, many selective colleges ask for letters of recommendation from the student's teachers, school counselor, or others (coaches, clergy, employer, even peers) who know the student well. What many students don't know, however, is that they have more opportunities to help the recommenders craft strong letters than they may realize.

Not all colleges ask for recommendations, and those that do will specify how many letters they'd like to see and whether or not those letters are optional. For example, in a recent application season, the University of Iowa did not *require* any teacher letters of recommendation but gave the option for students to submit up to three. They did not require any additional recommendations from the "others" group either but provided the option for students to submit three. So, a student could choose to submit no recommendations at all, or up to six recommendations total. When given the option, it's always better to provide at least two recommendations to help support the student's candidacy; don't skip them just because they are "optional." Villanova University, on the other hand, requires one teacher recommendation and does not give the student the option to submit any beyond that.

TEACHER RECOMMENDATIONS

To make sure they have their bases covered, students should request at least two, and possibly three, letters of recommendation from their teachers. That way, if one of the three teachers doesn't get it written and submitted on time, the student will still have two ready to go. Ideally, they'll ask their teachers in May or June of junior year so that the teachers can pre-plan, or even pre-write, the recommendations over the summer break.

If that timing is not possible, then asking early in senior year will work (but not the first week of school when teachers are busy with the logistics of getting the academic year started). Students who wait to ask until a week (or a day!) before the recommendations are due might be turned down, as teachers are not required to write these letters. If teachers agree to write one in a pinch, the student may get a letter that won't be as enthusiastic as it might otherwise be.

Junior year teachers are usually the best ones to ask for recommendations. They've known the student for an entire year (as opposed to the senior year teachers who are just getting to know the students), and they've known the student at their most mature, academically. Freshman year teachers may have known the student longer, but their insights into the student's academic capabilities will reflect that younger version of the student.

In addition, students who know what they plan to study in college should ask for letters of recommendation from teachers in aligned subject areas. A student interested in journalism should ask for a letter from an English teacher, who can comment on the student's writing abilities. A student interested in engineering can ask for letters from their math and physics teachers. Asking for letters from very different disciplines (such as physics and English) can attest to the student's strengths in a broad range of academics.

In addition, it's very important for students to ask for recommendations from teachers who really like them! It's more important to get a glowing letter of recommendation from a teacher who is enthusiastic about the student, regardless of discipline, than a lackluster recommendation from a teacher in a target subject. Caveat: "Regardless of discipline" applies to core academic subjects: English, math, science, social studies, foreign language. No one should be getting a letter of recommendation from their P.E. teacher.

Pro Tip

Teachers who write recommendations for schools that use the Common Application portal (that's most of the selective four-year, private colleges in the U.S.) are asked to not only write a letter, but rate the student using a grid that asks about the following criteria:

- Academic achievements
- Intellectual promise
- Quality of writing
- Creative thought

- Faculty respect
- Disciplined habits
- Maturity
- Leadership
- Integrity
- Reaction to setbacks
- Concern for others
- Self-confidence
- Initiative
- Overall

For each of those items, teachers can check off a rating box as follows: no basis, below average, average, good (above average), very good (well above average), excellent (top 10%), outstanding (top 5%), and "one of the top few I've encountered in my career." Well-informed students who plan ahead and keep this list handy can actively work toward demonstrating their abilities in each of these areas over the course of their time in the teacher's classroom.

You can access a link to a PDF copy of this chart through this book's resources page, https://www.CollegePrepCounseling.com/resources.

HOW TO ASK

Students should ask for a letter of recommendation in person—and it should be an ask, not a command. That is, the student should not say, "I need you to write me a letter of recommendation," but instead should ask, "Would you please write me a letter of recommendation?" Teachers write these recommendations during their own time on evenings and weekends, and popular teachers spend hours getting them all done. Yet they do it year after year because they care about the students, so ask your student to be particularly gracious in this process.

If a teacher agrees to write the student a letter, have the student follow up with a packet of information that will help make the teacher's job easier. The packet should include a cover letter, the student's résumé, and any other forms—sometimes called a "brag packet"—that the school may give to the student to fill out. The student should, basically, give information to the teacher that will help the teacher write the caliber of recommendation that the student is hoping for.

How can students help the teacher write a strong recommendation? In the cover letter, the student should include information on what they hope to study in college. They can mention any particularly positive incidents or anecdotes they remember from being in class that might have made an impression on the teacher. They can also bring in any other information that the teacher could, in effect, weave into their recommendation.

Here's an example, with an "I remember working on …" anecdote tucked in:

Dear Mrs. Crumpetcorn,

Thank you again for being willing to write a letter of recommendation for my college applications. As you know, I'm interested in studying journalism, so your insights into my writing abilities and approach to writing would be very helpful to the colleges.

In your AP English Language class last year, we worked on the assignment about Mark Twain's *Life on the Mississippi*. I remember that, on my paper, you commented that you found my comparison of Twain's memories of river life to Jerome K. Jerome's *Three Men in a Boat* story of floating down the Thames in England to be particularly perceptive.

Your positive comments on my writing have encouraged me to continue learning about writing outside of the classroom. Last summer, I attended Northwestern University's Medill School of Journalism's five-week program for high school students and had a chance to learn more about what a journalist's work and life really look like, and I couldn't be more thrilled to pursue this as my major and career.

My earliest applications are due October 15, so, if at all possible, it would be great if you could submit your recommendation no later than October 8.

Thank you again for helping me, not only with this part of my college applications, but with my education as a whole.

Best regards,
Kaylee Cook

THE COUNSELOR RECOMMENDATION

While the teacher recommendations focus on who the student is in the classroom, the counselor recommendation is more focused on who the student is in the context of the greater school community. Is the student engaged in school activities through sports teams or through participation in clubs or student government? What is the student known for at the school?

Quite often, especially in large public schools, the school counselor may not really know much about the student for whom they are writing a recommendation. It's in the best interest of the student to develop some sort of rapport with the counselor well ahead of senior year. The student should introduce themselves, find reasons to check in every now and then during sophomore and junior years, and bring the counselor into their planning. For example, a high school junior might pop in to let the counselor know they are considering a career in law and ask whether the counselor has any recommendations for internships or summer activities that could help them explore that field. Once senior year rolls around, the counselor can speak to the student's initiative from early on and address their interest in various career fields.

Some counselors ask their students to fill out a set of forms (the aforementioned "brag packet") to help the counselor find out more about the student so they can write a stronger recommendation. If your student's school distributes these types of forms, have your student take time to answer the questions thoroughly and thoughtfully. The counselor may take cues from the language the student uses to work phrases, perspectives, and key concepts into the recommendation.

OTHER RECOMMENDERS

Some colleges allow recommendations from those who are not teachers or counselors. This might be a Scout leader, rabbi, priest, imam, sports coach, employer, or other adult with whom the student has worked. The student should feel that this person can write them a strong and enthusiastic letter of recommendation and add a perspective or insight into the student's character and abilities that wouldn't likely show up in a teacher or counselor recommendation.

Recommendations from a religious leader are particularly helpful for students applying to strongly religious colleges.

FERPA

FERPA stands for the Family Educational Rights and Privacy Act. In this situation, FERPA grants the student the right to read the letters of recommendation that the teachers write.

But there's a catch. Teachers like to feel free to write honestly, and knowing that the student might read the recommendation could color how and what they write. For this reason, most students choose to waive, or give up, their FERPA right to read the recommendations. I would guess that 99.9% of students waive their right to review the recommendations.

By waiving their rights, these students are assuring the teachers that they trust them to write something helpful, and the colleges can trust that the teachers are being completely honest. Students who choose *not* to waive their rights may very well raise red flags with both the teachers and the colleges that they are concerned about what the teachers might say. This would make the colleges wonder what the student is worried about, which could taint the whole process. So, my recommendation is for the student to choose to waive their FERPA rights.

KEY TAKEAWAYS

1) Chat with your student about which junior year teachers would write them the strongest recommendations. Make sure the subjects taught by the teachers (core subjects!) align with the student's subject-of-interest or potential major.

2) Encourage them to ask the teachers early, either toward the end of junior year or a few weeks after school starts in senior year.

3) Print the Teacher Recommendation grid from the Common App and post it somewhere it can stay front-of-mind for your student.

4) Support your student in coming up with anecdotes or ideas for the cover letter and brag packet that will be handed to the teacher to assist in writing the recommendation.

5) Discuss with your student whether to waive their FERPA right to review the recommendations.

6) Consider outside recommenders whose knowledge of the student would add insight and a deeper understanding of the applicant to the application package.

9

Demonstrated Interest

M any parents are surprised to learn that some colleges track who has signed up for newsletters and college information from the college's website. They use sophisticated technology to monitor whether prospective students are opening the emails the college is sending, clicking on the links, and spending time reviewing the contents of those emails. Basically, colleges are trying to gauge the student's level of interest in the school. Those of us in admissions call this "demonstrated interest." The schools are trying to measure how interested a student really is in enrolling in their school, and, if your student doesn't demonstrate sufficient interest in schools that track this parameter, they very well might not be offered admission, even if they are exceedingly qualified as an applicant.

When the college's representative visits a high school, they note which students show up, who seems interested, and who sends a thank-you note afterward. (Psst—those admissions reps who visit the high schools are usually the first ones to review the applications from that school's students.)

The colleges monitor who is following them on Instagram or TikTok (and may in turn spend time reviewing the student's account, so the student's posts should be free of anything that may raise red flags for the colleges). Essentially, colleges want to admit students who will accept their offer of admission and not admit students who aren't likely to enroll.

Let's say a college offers admission to 100 students, and only 20 of them accept the offer to enroll. That's a 20% yield. Another school offers admission to 100 students, and 87 of them accept the offer to enroll. That means a yield of 87%. Colleges like to have a high yield, which can increase their perceived value and provide a data point to brag about how desirable their college is, driving more students to apply.

If a college can encourage more students to apply without increasing the number of spots available in each incoming freshman class, then the college becomes more selective—that is, the student admission rate drops. A school that accepts 20% of applicants is more selective than a school that accepts 50% of applicants. Generally, the more selective a college, the higher it goes in the rankings. So, it's good business sense for the colleges to try to get as many applications as they can, and then turn down more students, therefore increasing their selectivity. This is awful for the students, especially for those who get letters from colleges saying, "We'd love for you to apply." Students read that as, "We'd love to have you at our college." But no, they usually only mean that they want the student to submit an application, not that they necessarily want to admit the student.

There is another dark side to all this. More and more colleges appear to be practicing "yield protection." They will deny admission to an outstanding student, thinking that the student will likely be admitted to (and enroll in) an even more selective or more prestigious school and, therefore, would be unlikely to enroll even if the school offers them admission. This is our best guess as to what happened to a student who was accepted at two of the most selective schools in the U.S. (Harvard and Yale) and denied at a school that was not as selective (Wesleyan). That's only one example, but in counseling circles, these stories pop up over and over.

In other words, schools will sometimes deny a very capable student a spot in their class so that the college can protect their yield percentage. That makes it really hard for students to create a balanced list of reach, target, and likely schools because they never know whether they'll get denied from a target or likely school simply because a college is practicing yield protection.

How can students keep from getting denied because of yield protection? That's where demonstrated interest comes in. If the school is within a few hours' drive of the student's home, has the student bothered to take the time to visit the campus for a tour and an information session? Has the student participated in any online events the college has hosted or attended a presentation when the college rep stopped in at their high school for a visit?

And, of course, the holy grail of demonstrated interest is submitting an application for Early Decision, which is binding. If the student is admitted Early Decision, they commit to enroll, thereby ensuring a 100% yield on those students for the college. I'll cover Early Decision and other admissions options in more detail in Chapter 14.

Most Ivy League and other ultra-selective ("highly rejective") schools don't bother with yield protection. Their yields are so high that they claim they don't track demonstrated interest because pretty much all the students who apply would enroll if accepted. In the past, it appeared that public colleges didn't track demonstrated interest, either (although I'm just starting to hear stories indicating that may be shifting). Private colleges sandwiched (in terms of selectivity) between the Ivy League and the state colleges are the ones most likely to pay attention to these small but meaningful "demonstrated interest" efforts on the part of the students.

I mentioned earlier that representatives from the colleges fan out across the country each fall, visiting high schools to meet potential applicants and chat with students about what their college offers. The school counselors are the ones who coordinate these visits and tell students which schools will be sending representatives and during which specific days and class periods:

COLLEGE REP VISITS

TUESDAY 11/2
   California Aeronautical - P.4
   UC Santa Barbara -P.5
WEDNESDAY 11/3
   University of Redlands -P.3
   Southern Utah University -P.4
   University of Alabama -P.6
THURSDAY 11/4
   Willamette University -P.3

Students should regularly check for any school visits from colleges on their list. The college representatives often have assigned territories and know the schools in those territories well. They'll also evaluate the applications from students applying from their territory, and they'll notice if the student has taken the time to attend the school visit and introduce themselves. They'll take note of which students write a follow-up email (or even a snail mail) thanking them for taking the time to visit the high school.

How do you know which of the colleges on the student's list track demonstrated interest? It's in the Common Data Set (the same document we looked at in the chapter on Financial Aid). But this time, we're interested in the chart in section C7. Here's an example:

C7 Relative importance of each of the following academic and nonacademic factors in your first-time, first-year, degree-seeking (freshman) admission decisions.

	Very Important	Important	Considered	Not Considered
Academic				
Rigor of secondary school record	X			
Class rank			X	
Academic GPA	X			
Standardized test scores			X	
Application Essay		X		
Recommendation(s)	X			
Nonacademic				
Interview			X	
Extracurricular activities		X		
Talent/ability			X	
Character/personal qualites		X		
First generation			X	
Alumni/ae relation			X	
Geographical residence		X	X	
State residency				X
Religious affiliation/commitment				X
Racial/ethnic status				X
Volunteer work		X		
Work experience		X		
Level of applicant's interest			X	

On the very last row it says, "Level of applicant's interest," and, at this college, they are paying attention. You'll probably notice that this chart also has other helpful nuggets of information, such as what factors the college deems "very important" and "important."

As a parent, you can help your student in this process by tracking down and collecting the C7 chart for each of the colleges on the student's final list (you'll find links to the Common Data Set for nearly 200 colleges at https://www. CollegePrepCounseling.com/resources). In addition, if the student has created a separate email account to use for admissions tests, college contacts, and college applications, and if they share the login information with you, you can help your student "demonstrate interest" by checking the email account often, opening the emails, and clicking on the links.

KEY TAKEAWAYS

1) Research the Common Data Set for each school on your student's list to find out which ones track demonstrated interest.

2) Make sure your student is getting updates from their counselor on which colleges are planning visits to the high school. They should attend every visit by representatives from colleges on their list.

3) Help the student keep up on the college emails by going into the for-college-only email account you've set up and opening the emails from the colleges on the student's list. Click on the links embedded in those emails, and keep your student posted about news or interesting information presented.

4) Make plans to visit schools on your student's list that are within a reasonable drive from your hometown.

10

Campus Visits

Campus visits let a student get a boots-on-the-ground sense of a college's vibe—the overall energy and attitudes of the students—and ultimately help them decide whether that school is somewhere they'd like to spend the next four years of their lives.

A college's website, while informative, is a highly curated work of public relations. Once on campus, the college can be seen without that media-marketing filter. Are the college's students rushing around with anxious looks on their faces or happily greeting one another and stopping to chat as they transition between classes? Do they seem to radiate a cheerful attitude or do they look a bit bored or disconnected? Obviously, each individual student will go through cycles of moods, but visitors should be able to get a feel for how the majority of students are moving through their day on campus.

Take the opportunity to talk to current students and ask them why they chose that college and what they like and don't like about the school. Have your student arrange to have a meal in the cafeteria, sit in on a class in their prospective major, and possibly even stay overnight with a friend who attends.

Sometimes, the diversity of students on campus can help a visitor determine whether they can find the people they feel they can connect with and relate to on campus. Do some of the students dress in a way that echoes your student's sense of style? Is your student comfortable with the racial and international diversity on campus or would they prefer to see more?

What is the campus attitude about LGBTQ students and does that jive with your student's views? I have plenty of clients who are not LGBTQ themselves, but they are strong allies and would not want to attend a campus where LGBTQ students felt unwelcome.

I'm not suggesting that a student seek out a college where they only find students like themselves. I am suggesting that a student should feel comfortable enough on the campus that they feel safe as they stretch their comfort zone to broaden their experiences and their views.

It's often easier to get a sense of how comfortable the student feels at a certain campus, and how much they like the entire campus environment, by paying the college a visit.

That said, visiting a bunch of colleges spread across the country can be both expensive and exhausting. I often recommend to my clients that they *do not* make a pilgrimage to visit reach schools that are a five-hour plane flight away from home. Students can travel to those schools if and when they are offered admission. At that point, they can visit the campus (I call this the "victory tour") and know that, if they love it and if the finances work out, it's an actual option for them to enroll.

There's nothing more difficult than having a student visit a reach school and utterly fall in love with it, making it their "one and only," when they have such a slim statistical chance of being admitted. I really want my clients to fall in love with *all* the colleges on their list, including the likely and target schools, and if the student and family don't even bother to visit those likely and target schools, the message is that those schools are somehow less worthy. This sets the student up for disappointment if they are not admitted to a highly selective school. Please, as one parent to another—cheer for all the schools on your student's list. Genuinely get behind them all because, if your inner soul is saying that "XYZ school is unworthy," your student will pick up on that. Remember, it's a huge win to even be in the game of applying to a four-year college. There is much to celebrate, and there can be great success for students in their lives even if it doesn't include a bumper sticker from an Ivy League university.

Parents of one of my recent clients decided to take him on a tour of Vanderbilt, a wonderful college to which he had essentially zero chance of getting in (his GPA was lower than that of nearly all admitted students). Of course, he *loved* it. Now what? Does he throw away his Early Decision option for a school that is almost guaranteed to not love him back? Thankfully, we found another reach school for him that he also loved (though it was less "reachy" than Vanderbilt) where we thought his Early Decision commitment might pop him in, and that's exactly what happened.

Visiting colleges within about a three-hour drive of the student's home can be easier to arrange than flying across the country. In fact, if a school is within a half day's drive from the student's hometown and the student *hasn't* bothered to visit, the college may note that (if they are tracking "demonstrated interest," as discussed in the last chapter) and assume the student is not seriously considering enrolling if they are admitted. That may make the college hesitate to offer the student a spot (unless the student is from a low-income area or otherwise indicates that they do not have the means to make a visit, in which case the colleges will not hold it against them in the admissions process).

I'll sometimes recommend that students visit nearby colleges of various student population sizes—small (5,000 students or fewer), medium (5,000–10,000 students), large (10,000–20,000 students), and extra-large (20,000 or more)—just to get a sense of what a campus of those sizes feels like. For example, I often recommend to my San Diego students that they take a weekend afternoon to visit either Point Loma Nazarene University (3,200 students), University of San Diego (8,200 students), UC San Diego (36,000 students) or San Diego State University (34,000 students). Visiting local colleges helps them build a baseline understanding of what to expect from college visits and gives them more background against which to evaluate the colleges that actually make it onto their list.

Don't visit on days when the college students are on breaks (as the campus will be emptied of students) or when they are studying for finals, when the campus atmosphere is likely to be uncharacteristically tense and gloomy.

THE OFFICIAL CAMPUS TOUR AND INFORMATION SESSION

Most colleges allow visitors to sign up for an official 30-minute information session and 90-minute campus tour. There is usually a form on each college's website (in the Admissions section, under "Visit" or "Campus Visit" or "Campus Tours") that allows you (yes, this is one of those things you as a parent can do to help your student in this process) to pre-register for a visit on a certain day and time. You'll often see these two-hour information session/campus tour combinations offered at 10:00 a.m. and 2:00 p.m. Some colleges only offer these on weekdays, which is problematic for high schoolers who have classes to attend on those days. Check your student's school schedule for teacher in-service days or other days when their high school is not in session, and try to arrange for campus visits on those days.

For efficiency, where you can, try to visit two colleges that are near one another on the same day—one during the morning session and one during the afternoon session. Have your student take pictures of the campus and the tour guide to help jog their memory later on. You and your student may very well find that, at first, the colleges and campuses blur together, and it may be hard to remember which colleges had what features. It's super important for your student to take notes during the information session and jot down impressions afterward to keep track of notable programs, opportunities, facilities, or resources at the college, which could range from the Mortimer Rare Book Collection at Smith College to the Roll Tide Water Slide at the University of Alabama. As the process goes on and the student spends more time unearthing the nitty gritty details that they love about each college, the blurred impressions should begin to clarify. Also, keep a record of the dates you visited each school. Some schools will ask for the date of your visit on the application forms.

Another reason to register for the official tour and info session is to ensure that the colleges know you were there for a visit. Again, this is part of demonstrated interest and gets you on the college's email and snail mail lists. It opens the channels of communication with the college and puts your student on their radar.

Having the student ask questions in the information session and on the tours is expected (although no one is watching to see whether a particular student did or did not ask a question). Questions should be focused on information not readily available on the website (such as, how hard it is to get the classes the student wants, how the school determines who gets on-campus housing if they can't accommodate 100% of the students, and if the college has a program to facilitate internships or mentorship opportunities for the students). If, as parents, you have the opportunity to join a different tour than your student, take it! Then you can ask all the questions you want, and your student can feel free to ask their own questions without any concern about parental interference or judgment.

One more thing: if the college tour doesn't include a visit to the career counseling center, be sure that you and your student drop in on your own before or after the tour. Find out if they help arrange internships for the students, provide individual career counseling, review résumés, and train students how to negotiate a salary. Find out how many job fairs they put on each year, how many businesses have booths at those fairs, and the names of the businesses that regularly attend.

Internships during college, by the way, are critically important for a student's long-term outcome from their time in college. According to the *Great Jobs, Great Lives: The 2014 Gallup-Purdue Index Report*, participating in internships that were specifically related to content the students were learning in their academics, working on long-term projects (a semester or more), and active engagement in extracurricular activities all pointed to better results for students when they enter the workforce: "Feeling supported and having deep learning experiences means everything when it comes to long-term outcomes for college graduates."

You can access the link to the Gallup website and the full downloadable report by visiting this book's resources page at https://www.CollegePrepCounseling.com/resources.

─────────────── **Pro Tip** ───────────────

I mentioned taking notes during the information session. In particular, ask your student to pay attention to the unique qualities of the school that the admissions personnel are emphasizing during the talk. With only 30 minutes, they are going to highlight those aspects of their college that they think will make the biggest impression on prospective students. Remember, they want students to apply, and they want enough students to enroll to fill all the available spots. If your student takes good notes during the information session, they can echo some of those highlights in their "Why This College?" essay and align their application to the aspects of the college that the college is most proud of.

_____

MAKE TIME FOR A VIRTUAL VISIT FIRST

At some point before the day of the official visit (or even before scheduling those), sit down with your student and spend an hour or so doing a "virtual visit" from the school's website.

You'll be able to look at (and possibly print out) a map of the campus to get a sense of what's there, and you can preview what you'll see on your actual tour. You can mark any specific buildings, departments, or campus highlights your student wants to make sure they see (even if the official tour doesn't include those spaces), and you can get a sense of whether the buildings, grounds, and general environment align with what your student is looking for. If your student finds, after going through a virtual visit, that the campus is not a good match after all, then you can cancel the campus tour and find another school to investigate. It's much easier to do a first pass through a virtual tour than to spend the time to get to the college and tour for two hours if your student can quickly decide from a virtual visit that they're not actually interested.

By the way, brace yourself. Students can be extremely fickle about which colleges make it onto their list and which don't. I've had students who steadfastly refused to even get out of the family car when they arrived at a campus for a visit. As much as I might think it's fun and exciting for students to visit campuses, the entire college search and application process—and college visits—can sometimes trigger anxiety or dread or who-knows-what in a student.

Even if you've spent hours getting them to a campus, please let them make this call. Love and support them. Let them know that you've got their back even if you are disappointed or feeling frustrated. Try to focus on gratitude for the time spent with your teen before they head to college and they are no longer at home on a daily basis. This really is the student's journey, and some-times they just "know" that it's not a good fit or they're simply not ready to take the next step—literally! It may not make sense to you, but maybe, this one time, they need your grace and understanding to just let it go (yes, this could be problematic if this is your financial and admissions safety school, in which case you'll have to use your parental judgment on how best to move forward). Sending hugs, oh fellow parent of a teen!

KEY TAKEAWAYS

1) Take a virtual tour of the college before setting out to see the campus in person.

2) Take time to visit the target and likely schools on the list. Help the student fall in love with those schools in addition to their reach schools.

3) If two of the colleges are in the same vicinity, you can usually knock out two campus visits in one day (one in the morning and one in the afternoon).

4) Make sure to register on the college's website for the official information session and tour so that the admissions department knows you were there.

5) Be sure to stop by the career counseling center to ask questions.

6) Try to be gracious and understanding with your student if they freeze up and don't want to follow through with the tour.

11

Essays: The Big Picture

For many students, the most difficult part of the college application process is writing the seemingly endless essays. It's easy to understand why. The essays ask the students to write about themselves. The best ones help the admissions readers learn who the student is and, even better, feel positive enough about the applicant that they want to see that student on their campus the following year. The essays are a chance for the student's personality to jump off the page. They offer an opportunity for the student to breathe life into an application that would otherwise be reduced to flat and impersonal data—GPA, test scores, and a few descriptive lines about their activities.

It's precisely this first-person, self-reflective aspect of the college essays that makes them so hard to write. Most students have been told not to use the first-person "I" in an essay—which is the case for academic writing—but this personal college application essay format requires it.

In addition, most students aren't used to thinking about their own lives and reflecting on who they are now, how they grew to become that person, and their hopes for the future. That mature self-reflection, however, is one key to writing a great essay. In addition, students aren't used to sharing those inner thoughts with some unknown admissions officer who can help sway a college's decision in their favor. The stakes are high and the task feels uncomfortable, so the anxiety rises, and it gets worse as the fall deadlines approach.

Rather than having the whole essay be about the musings in their head, however, the best essays are anchored by a detailed, slice-of-life story that gives structure to the essay. This should be some specific anecdote or incident that helps the reader get to know the student and how they've behaved or reacted to a situation. This also gives the writer something specific to reflect on.

I often recommend that students muster the confidence to share what I call their "soft underbelly," a situation or time when things went sideways and they had to figure out how to course-correct. As a reader, it's easy to cheer on an underdog and empathize with a student who's had something go awry (and then fixed it). The opposite approach—boastful stories from students who are trying too hard to impress by their perfection and attitude of "I'm better than everyone else, pick me!"—can put off the reader. In my essay class, I show a picture of the over-muscled, arrogant, and thoroughly unlikeable character Gaston from *Beauty and the Beast* and warn the students: "Don't be Gaston." Bottom line: the students should tell a story that helps the reader get to know them as relatable, likable, interesting, and memorable.

Parents often ask me how they can help in this process. My best advice is to help your student brainstorm topics—those incidents and situations that can be the foundation of the essays—over the dinner table or during car rides. Help them find or remember those micro-moments in their lives that can serve as the kernel of a story. Beyond that, I recommend that parents stay one step removed. Writing these essays is a rite of passage that the student must endure without their parents being in the weeds with them, as parents can't help but bring the weight of their own expectations, hopes, and preconceptions into the process. It's often very difficult for parents to resist the temptation to just "go in and fix it" as they read a student's essay drafts, but, too often, incorporating those fixes means losing the student's authentic voice, language, and syntax in the process.

WRITE THE ESSAYS EARLY

The key to keeping essay-writing anxiety to a minimum? Have the student start writing early. Let me repeat that for emphasis: *start early!*

How early? Every June for more than a decade (with the exception of 2020 during the COVID-19 pandemic), I've headed to the desert town of Temecula, California, for the weekend. I go at the invitation of my colleagues and friends, Tom and Ardeth Meier, who hire me to teach their 80 or so rising seniors the art and science of how to write amazing college application essays.

The course runs three hours on Saturday afternoon and then continues for three hours on Sunday afternoon. In between, the students have time to process what they've learned and start jotting down ideas for topics they will write about and how they might present those topics for maximum impact.

Generally, the students slump into the room on Saturday, usually not overly excited to be starting a six-hour course on essay writing. And that's okay! By the end of the two sessions, they get it. They are full of energy and ideas and enthusiasm. It's actually fun, which surprises many of the students in the class. The turnaround in students' attitudes and outlook over the course of the training is one reason I love teaching that class.

Because the course is taught in June, these students have the whole summer to think about and write their essays. The goal is to get at least six core essays—the main essay, one on community, one on impact, one on self-identity, one on "why this major," and at least one "why our college" essay—done before their senior year starts (we'll detail each of those in the next chapter). If they can do that, their entire application season becomes much less stressful because those core essays can then be modified to answer multiple prompts from any number of colleges.

How many total essays will the student need to write? It depends on the number of colleges they are applying to and the essays those colleges want to see. The most selective colleges have between three and eight supplemental essays and short-answer questions to which the student will need to respond. Other colleges, such as Case Western Reserve University, require only the student's main Common Application essay. And some colleges don't require any essays at all.

A few years back, one of my late-start students—she began working with me in October of her senior year—was applying to 16 very selective colleges. She came in with a list of 41 essays she needed to write for those applications, and she was panicking. We sat down for a strategy session and looked at each of the essay prompts—the questions the essays are supposed to address—and grouped them by topic. The prompts were all different, but those core essay themes popped up over and over.

My student ended up needing to write only (okay, "only" here is relative) about 14 essays, several of which were core essays that she revised slightly to fit each individual college's prompts.

TELL A GOOD STORY

After reading hundreds of application essays every year, I can tell you that only about 5% of application essays are truly outstanding. These essays give us information about who the writer is—a likable, interesting, thoughtful young adult—through a well-crafted, small story that shows, rather than tells, what they've learned about themselves thus far in their lives. Another 5% are so poorly crafted or inappropriate that they'd immediately remove the student from the college's consideration (we are able to catch these for our clients and pivot the student before those essays ever get to the colleges). The rest of the 90% are simply ... typical. They neither help nor hurt the student's application, and those are the ones we try to help the students level up.

You want to hear about the worst ones, don't you? Okay, let's start with those. There was one student who talked about "... reading *Harry Potter* on those long visits to the bathroom" (no reader wants to envision a student in the bathroom). To make it worse, he then talked about his thoughts of using the forbidden curses from that book series—the Cruciatus torture curse and the Avada kedavra killing curse—on those whom he dislikes. Not a stretch to understand how this would be a major red flag to any admissions office. That essay was what we would call a "do-over." We stop it in its tracks, so it never sees the light of day in an admissions office. Then we help the student think up a different topic to write about (and yes, if we think there's a worrisome mental health issue, we'll bring it to the attention of the parents).

Another student misunderstood what selective, prestigious colleges are looking for. He must have thought the admissions officers were a bunch of pretentious snobs … and he was willing to grovel to land on their campus: "The knowledge I will gain at (college name) will excel me above my other coworkers and place me among the elite in order to strive to the top." Just … no.

More than a decade ago, one of the students I worked with was aiming for UC Berkeley and Stanford. He insisted that those schools want to admit leaders (in that, he was correct). But his vision of what a leader was seemed off to me.

He was his Boy Scout troop's senior patrol leader. His essay discussed a troop hike he led to a mountain peak near his home. The whole essay was about how he was the first up the mountain, charging ahead of all the other scouts. I guess he thought that being the leader meant being in front or being first?

I suggested that he might want to talk about how he checked on the younger scouts to make sure they were doing okay on the hike, how he perhaps reminded the others to stay hydrated and watch for snakes on the trail. But no. He insisted on writing only about being first up the mountain. Honestly, he just sounded self-centered and arrogant, which is not the type of leader any schools are looking for. He ignored my advice, sent in the "I was first to the top" essay … and was denied at both schools. Was he denied *only* because of the essay? Not likely (although we'll never know for sure), but that essay certainly didn't help him in the process.

How about the average essays? Those are stories that rehash universal experiences many college-bound high school students can write about. A few of the topics that often hit college reviewers with dismay include:

- "I threw the winning touchdown pass."
- "I broke my arm/leg playing sports and my recovery was a challenge."
- "Someone I love died of cancer, so I want to be a doctor."
- "My parents divorced and my grades dropped."
- "I went to another country and built a school/house/ orphanage and realized just how good I have it back home."
- "I took a hard course and then had to study harder to get a better grade."
- "I had to study from home during COVID."

It's not that the student can't write about any of those topics, but if they do choose one of those, they need to be very careful to bring in details and a different angle so that the story is fresh to the reader and unique to them—otherwise it will get relegated to the pile of average essays.

I once had a student in my essay course write about a trip to Botswana to help build an orphanage (yes, I rolled my eyes when I read the first paragraph of the first draft and thought, *Oh no, one of* those *essays*). He had written about living in "a typical African home" and how he was amazed to finally understand how fortunate he was back home in a suburban U.S. town.

When I met with him to discuss the essay, I asked him to, first of all, acknowledge that Africa is an entire continent comprised of more than 50 countries. The vastly disparate peoples include the Sahara's Berber nomads in their tents, the indigenous tribes of the Congo living in rainforest huts, and the modern-day Egyptians in Cairo living in high-rise apartments. The point I was trying to make to the student was that there is no such thing as a "typical African home"—that overgeneralization made him sound tone deaf to the enormous cultural variations within all those countries. I asked him to make the story less generic and more specifically his.

He did an amazing job revising the essay to describe the actual home in which he stayed with a local family, to name one of the orphans he had befriended, and to reflect on larger lessons learned beyond "I realized how lucky I am." That student ended up at Harvard, which I suspect may very well not have happened if he had submitted the first draft of that essay.

And the best essays of all? Those are delightful little gems, stories where the student has been courageous enough to share personal detail about something that perhaps didn't work out at first, but the student was able to make it right as they evolved in maturity and outlook. These essays are memorable and filled with little groups of two- or three-word phrases that show how the writer sees the world a little bit differently from everyone else. For example, the girl who described the sounds of Las Vegas as "aurally intoxicating" or another who wrote about her unibrow, calling it "the lush national forest burgeoning above the bridge of my nose" and "a fuzzy, built-in sweater."

One student magically wove together a story of struggling to get the notes right in a piano piece, when suddenly she was inspired in her playing by the rhythm of a poem she read in English class. Another student discussed challenges faced as an ethnic minority in a majority white school, and how she came to accept herself, told through the story of a small but seminal incident in her life. One discussed the hard work of raising his own money to buy a broken-down car, then taking it apart down to the bolts and spending a year fixing it up again. These stories are full of authenticity, confidence without arrogance, and clever word choices. They display the student's ability to let the story carry the weight for them of who they are, what they think, and what they value.

If your student is looking for insight or inspiration on how these types of essays sound, have them listen to a few episodes of the podcast *This I Believe* (ThisIBelieve.org) or the podcast *The Moth* (themoth.org). Both have wonderful examples of people telling their stories in this first-person format.

KEY TAKEAWAYS

1) Start early. Before the end of junior year, students should check out the essay prompts for several of the colleges on their list.

2) It takes time to write thoughtful, self-reflective essays. Help your student brainstorm stories and incidents from their life that might work as essay topics. They should start writing in the summer and get through as many essays as possible to avoid a painfully stressful fall.

3) Listen to the podcasts *This I Believe* and *The Moth* for ideas on how to tell a story and how to shape a first-person narrative.

12

Essays: The Six Core Essays

In the last chapter, I mentioned the six core essays the student ought to write before senior year starts. The goal should be to get these core essays done over the summer before their senior year. Working on them over the summer takes the pressure off trying to tackle them in the fall when there's extra deadline pressure (not to mention homework for senior-level classes), and it gives them the gift of time to develop the best stories.

Students who have their college list finalized in early summer can create an account on the Common App and fish out last year's essay prompts to see what each college normally asks. These prompts do change on occasion, but if the student waits to gather the prompts until the Common App is updated in August, they'll lose all that time in June and July to move forward on the essays. Yes, they may end up writing an extra essay or two, but that's better than trying to jam too many essays into too short a window after August.

Let's go through each of the core essays so your student knows what to expect.

CORE ESSAY #1: THE "MAIN" ESSAY

Most students will apply to at least one college that uses the Common Application as their online application portal. We'll talk more about portals in the next chapter, but, for now, know that the student will need to write one "main" essay for the Common Application.

This essay will go to all their Common App schools, so it's critical that it be written well and that it helps the colleges learn about some key aspects of who the student is. It also needs to convey that the student is competent, interesting, and likable.

A lot of my students are shocked to learn just how short college application essays can be. This main Common App essay has a word limit of 650 (and ought to be no fewer than 500 words). The student can select their essay topic from among seven prompts that don't vary much from year to year. The prompt options include asking about the student's background, lessons they've learned from obstacles, a time when the student questioned a belief or idea, what someone has done for them that's made them happy, an accomplishment or event that sparked personal growth, a topic they find engaging, or a topic of the student's choice. You can Google "Common App essay prompts" for the exact wording.

A quick clarification: I mentioned that most students send the same Common Application main essay to each of their schools that use that platform, but it is actually possible to write several versions that go to different schools. Most students prefer not to do that extra writing, so I won't get into the details of how to do that here.

I encourage students to write this main Common App essay first so that, when the student considers what to write about in the supplementary essays, they can then find a subject that complements and doesn't overlap with the topic of the main essay.

CORE ESSAY #2: WHY OUR COLLEGE?

Remember in Chapter 9 when I talked about the importance of "demonstrated interest" on the part of the student? The "Why Our College?" essay is one way the colleges measure how much the student knows about their particular institution. They want to know exactly *why* their school interests the student.

When a college asks this, the student must give answers that are absolutely and uniquely specific to that *one* college and do so in a way that shows they've really done their research on that institution. If they write an essay in which they can cross out the college name and replace it with another college name and the essay still makes sense, then they haven't done their job.

Here's an example of what *not* to write:

I've always wanted to study biology, and I know that ABC College offers that major.

Do you see how you can cross out "ABC College" and write in "XYZ College" and it wouldn't make any difference to the sentence? It doesn't make any difference to the sentence, but it makes a big difference to ABC College when they are thinking about whether to offer the student admission.

Instead, the student should aim for something much more specific, such as:

> *Harvard's extensive collection of more than 403,000 specimens of brachiopods at the Museum of Comparative Zoology would allow me to continue my studies of the effects of ocean acidification on these marine organisms.*

Here's another statement that is too generic to earn points for the writer:

> *I've always wanted to go to college in Boston.*

Boston has about 35 colleges, so this is not making a connection with any one specific college.

Instead, try something like:

> *At Emerson, I could host a radio show on WERS or perhaps even produce a field show on The Emerson Channel.*

THE *EASIEST ESSAYS EVER* ZIPPER TECHNIQUE

I teach an online essay course called *Easiest Essays Ever,* and, in it, I describe my Zipper Technique. Students need to write "Why Our College" essays as though they were zipping a zipper. One side of the zipper is the student—their interests in a major, in extracurricular activities, in research, in a career. On the other side of the zipper is the college—its specific resources, its clubs, its professors and programs. The essay should gracefully weave back and forth between the student's interests and the college's offerings, zipping the two together until the reader can precisely picture how that student would take advantage of the opportunities available on campus.

The student should start the zipper with what they are looking for in a college and then write about a resource at the college that aligns with what they are seeking. Then the essay goes back to the student—a field they'd like to study. Then back to the college—a professor who is well-known in that field. Back to the student—a club in which they'd like to participate, and then back to the college—the chapter of that club on its campus.

For this to work, students need to dig deep into the college's website. Find a professor whose work interests them. Perhaps they'd like to take a class from this person or apply to work in their lab or as some sort of assistant. Have them find at least one major or program that has something that piques their interest. Find an extracurricular activity they'd participate in on campus.

When the student can put those sorts of campus-specific details into an essay and describe how those details fit with the student's background and goals, they'll help the admissions team envision the student on their campus and understand how the student would take advantage of the unique resources that college has to offer.

Most "Why Our College?" essays are quite short, between 100 and 400 words. There's no room for fluff. The student should make the point to show how the college aligns with what the student is searching for. They should avoid telling the admissions readers facts they already know about their own institution ("… with its prestigious programs and 12:1 student-to-faculty ratio …").

The downside of these types of essays is that students can only pre-write, or at least pre-plan, their half of the zipper. The college-specific part of the zipper must be customized for each college on their list.

CORE ESSAY #3: WHAT HAVE YOU DONE TO MAKE YOUR COMMUNITY A BETTER PLACE?

What has your student done to improve the lives of those in their school, church, or civic community? Colleges predict a student's involvement on their campus by gauging how involved the student is in their hometown or high school community. Students should be able to write about this topic with enthusiasm and energy, giving details and data regarding their impact.

Here are some example prompts asked in a recent application cycle. Notice the similarities among these prompts. If a student has a story to tell that addresses this general topic, then that story can easily be modified to answer each specific prompt and word count.

- **MIT:** At MIT, we bring people together to better the lives of others. MIT students work to improve their communities in different ways, from tackling the world's biggest challenges to being a good friend. Describe one way in which you have contributed to your community, whether in your family, the classroom, your neighborhood, etc. (250 words)
- **Occidental:** Oxy's central mission emphasizes the value of community amidst diversity. What do you value in a community and how do you see your perspectives and life experiences enhancing it? (300 words)
- **Swarthmore:** Swarthmore students' worldviews are often forged by their prior experiences and exposure to ideas and values. Our students are often mentored, supported, and developed by their immediate context—in

their neighborhoods, communities of faith, families, and classrooms. Reflect on what elements of your home, school, or community have shaped you or positively impacted you. How have you grown or changed because of the influence of your community? (250 words)

- **University of Michigan, Ann Arbor:** Everyone belongs to many different communities and/or groups defined by (among other things) shared geography, religion, ethnicity, income, cuisine, interest, race, ideology, or intellectual heritage. Choose one of the communities to which you belong and describe that community and your place within it. (300 words)

- **University of Washington, Seattle:** Our families and communities often define us and our individual worlds. Community might refer to your cultural group, extended family, religious group, neighborhood or school, sports team or club, co-workers, etc. Describe the world you come from and how you, as a product of it, might add to the diversity of the University of Washington. (300 words)

As a parent, you can support your student by showing them how to keep a running list of their activities. If you are doing this exercise in the middle of junior year, they may have forgotten some of their activities from early high school, so work together to make sure nothing has been forgotten. Help them see and, if possible, quantify their impact (for example, total funds raised, number of items delivered, number of people helped). These not only go on the résumé and on the activities list but can also spark ideas for essay topics.

CORE ESSAY #4: TELL US WHY YOU'VE CHOSEN YOUR MAJOR

College admissions officers can learn a lot about an applicant in these types of essays. Sometimes they are genuinely curious about how the student came to consider their potential major (students are often asked to indicate their first-choice major on the college applications). They want to know if the student is articulate about the field and can speak from any real experience. They also are looking for alignment between what the student claims is their major of interest and the coursework and extracurricular activities the student has participated in.

Here are some example prompts:

- **California Lutheran University:** What interests you about your intended major? (250 words max)
- **Georgia Tech (Georgia Institute of Technology):** Why do you want to study your chosen major specifically at Georgia Tech? (300 words max)
- **Lehigh University:** With the understanding that some students will change colleges at Lehigh after the first year, please briefly describe why you chose to apply to the first-choice college or major that you listed above. (200 words max)
- **Loyola Marymount University:** Please briefly state your reason for wishing to attend LMU and/or how you came to select your major. (500 words max)
- **Purdue University:** Briefly discuss your reasons for pursuing the major you have selected. (100 words max)
- **Rice University:** Please explain why you wish to study in the academic areas you selected above. (150 words)

- **University of Colorado, Boulder:** Please share a bit more about your academic interests. What do you hope to study at CU Boulder? What has inspired your interests in this area? Or, if you are undecided, what area(s) of study are you considering? Think about your prior/ current coursework, extracurricular activities, work/ volunteer experiences, future goals, or anything else that has shaped your interests. (250 words max)

Alignment among the different elements of an application shows authenticity in what the student is saying; misalignment is a red flag. For example, sometimes students interested in competitive majors know that their choice may make it harder for them to be admitted to a college, so a few students try to get admitted via a less competitive major and then hope to transfer into their prefered major once they are on campus.

This can be true for, say, students who are pre-med (which is not actually a major but a sequence of specific classes required for medical school admissions). If a student indicates that they are pre-med or interested in biology on the application forms, the college may view their application against the applications of other pre-meds and hold them to a higher standard than they would for applicants with another interest. So, some pre-med students dodge the biology or biochemistry majors in favor of, say, art or classical studies, which they think will help their admissions chances.

However, if a student claims to be interested in majoring in classics (learning to speak and read Greek and/or Latin, studying culture and literature from ancient times) but none of their extracurricular activities or classes has anything to do with the classics, the admissions officers will pick up on that misalignment.

Similarly, let's say a student states that they *are* pre-med, but the student has no foundational experience during summers or in their extracurricular activities where they have, in essence, been around that field to try it on for size. That student's application will not be as strong as the application of a student who volunteered at a hospital, did an internship at a medical lab, and volunteered to assist in COVID-19 vaccination clinics—in other words, the student who has been around people working daily in the field and has a more grounded sense of what the field entails.

CORE ESSAY #5: TELL US ABOUT ONE OF YOUR EXTRACURRICULAR ACTIVITIES

Sometimes this essay aligns with the "What have you done to make your community a better place?" essay. The student can write one essay that answers both prompts and use them for different colleges. This one is specifically asking about something outside of academics that is important to the student.

Here are some example prompts:

- **Stanford University:** Briefly elaborate on one of your extracurricular activities, a job you hold, or responsibilities you have for your family. (50 words)
- **University of Portland:** Please briefly describe one of your extracurricular activities or work experiences. (250 words max)
- **MIT:** We know you lead a busy life, full of activities, many of which are required of you. Tell us about

something you do simply for the pleasure of it. (250 words max)

- **Princeton:** Briefly elaborate on an activity, organization, work experience, or hobby that has been particularly meaningful to you. (Please respond in about 150 words)
- **Harvard:** Your intellectual life may extend beyond the academic requirements of your particular school. Please use the space below to list additional intellectual activities that you have not mentioned or detailed elsewhere in your application. These could include, but are not limited to, supervised or self-directed projects not done as schoolwork, training experiences, online courses not run by your school, or summer academic or research programs not described elsewhere. (150 words)

CORE ESSAY TOPIC #6: HOW DO YOU IDENTIFY?

This is a new one in the last few years. This is an opportunity for students to discuss their race, ethnicity, gender identity, sexual orientation, or another aspect of how they identify. Sometimes this essay is optional, but sometimes it is required.

Examples:

- **University of Colorado, Boulder:** At the University of Colorado Boulder, no two Buffs are alike. We value difference and support equity and inclusion of all students and their many intersecting identities. Pick one of your unique identities and describe its significance. (650 words)
- **University of North Carolina, Chapel Hill:** Describe an aspect of your identity (for example, your religion, culture, race, sexual or gender identity, affinity group,

etc.). How has this aspect of your identity shaped your life experiences thus far? (200–250 words)

- **Lewis and Clark University:** At Lewis & Clark, we strive to be an inclusive community. Reflecting on a part of your identity (for example, your culture, race, ability status, sex, gender identity/expression, sexual orientation, national origin, political affiliation, religion, age, or veteran status, etc.), share with us an experience where you engaged with difference. (300 words)
- **Chapman:** Every Chapman student holds multiple identities that create the diverse fabric of our community. Our committee would like to hear about the intersectionality of your identities and how those have played a crucial role in your life. (200 words max)
- **Duke:** Duke University seeks a talented, engaged student body that embodies the wide range of human experience; we believe that the diversity of our students makes our community stronger. If you'd like to share a perspective you bring or experiences you've had that would help us understand you better, perhaps a community you belong to or your family or cultural background, we encourage you to do so here. Real people are reading your application, and we want to do our best to understand and appreciate the real people applying to Duke. (250-word limit)

HELPING THE STUDENT GET STARTED

It is one of the ironies of college admissions that students who claim to be ready for the academic rigors of college—which include the ability to manage their time and pace themselves through long research projects—nearly universally procrastinate on writing their college application essays. But like all big projects that seem daunting at first, each college essay is best tackled in several small steps over a long period of time.

The first step, and the one that causes the most consternation in students, is to figure out what topic to write about. The trick is for your student to take the time to reflect on themselves. Many students find it uncomfortable to sit quietly and think back on their own lives and try to tease out where and how, exactly, they came to be the people that they are. But that is exactly what the colleges want to know—who they are outside of the grades and test scores, how they think, and what they value.

For students who feel stuck, I suggest they create a timeline of their lives and try to pinpoint any moment—a conversation, an experience—that may not have seemed so significant at the time but on reflection somehow changed or more clearly defined who they are and where they are going in life. Remember, it's never too late to have an epiphany, and epiphanies can often be good fodder for application essay topics.

Once they have a few moments written down, I ask them to try jam writing—writing as if no one were looking or editing or caring about spelling, punctuation, or grammar. Just tell the story of that moment. If they find one where the memories or thoughts flow rather quickly, they may be onto something.

The second step is to use the good bits from the jam writing session to launch the actual writing of the essay. The student's choice of approach, language, organization, and suspense (or lack thereof) are all fair game for the admissions officer's complimentary (or critical) eye. A small story always works best when writing an application essay. It makes the essay more interesting for the reader, certainly more interesting than reading an essay that is simply a listing of the student's high school accomplishments.

In my essay course, we often talk about how to organize the story in a dynamic way—almost never following chronological order—and we read sample essays that show these strategies in action. The students write, get feedback, rewrite, and get more feedback. We go back and forth several times until the students get their essays just right.

Students should plan to write at least two drafts of each essay before they get to a final version. They should give themselves the gift of time to write a decent draft and then set it aside for a week. They'll be amazed when they go back to it how quickly they'll see what needs to be strengthened and what needs to be pruned.

By the second draft, students can get input from one or two language-savvy adults—perhaps an English teacher or school counselor. Unfortunately, more often than not, you as the parent aren't going to be able to give them the objective input they would accept and find helpful. Parents should be mindful that even good advice is no good if it changes the tone of the essay into something that doesn't sound like the student.

After this next round of revisions, the student should again let the essay sit on the shelf for another week or two, and then they'll be ready to read it again one last time with fresh eyes and create a final version. Then, and only then, should they do a final proofread for spelling, punctuation, and grammar, each of which must be as close to perfect as possible in the final essay the student submits to the colleges.

If your teen wants extra support with the essays, my *Easiest Essays Ever* online course offers students a series of tasks that breaks down the writing process into manageable bits to help overcome the temptation to procrastinate. My counseling team and I review the essays and give the student feedback on multiple versions of each of the essays they write in the course, after which I run the best version past a professional proofreader for a final check.

Please encourage your student to tackle their essays in the summer. Essays written under the stress of deadline pressure almost never show the student's best work.

A WORD OF CAUTION

Sometimes, parents get so wound up by the idea that their child's successful future is riding on their admission to College A or College B that they lose themselves in the frenzy—perhaps not quite to the degree of the Varsity Blues admission scandal of 2019, but along those same lines. Under no circumstances should you as the parent write your student's essay for them. First and foremost, you will utterly undermine your student by doing so. It's as if you're saying, "This is too important, and I don't trust you to do the job well on your own."

Second, writing someone else's personal essay is, of course, highly unethical and dishonest, and these parents are basically role modeling to their student how to cheat. The parent's integrity goes out the window.

That should be the end of the story, but I'll go on because I've seen it happen (including last year, when a student who was struggling with her essays suddenly showed up with five of them ready to go, all written with the voice of a 50-year-old and gushing about the wonderful influence of her parents, with the last paragraph talking about, "And when she arrives on campus, she will ...").

Remember: college admissions officers have read enough of these essays that they can sniff out a parent essay a mile away (even when the parents are careful enough to not mix up their pronouns or inject self-praise into the text) and it can actually *hurt* a student's chances of admission to send in that essay, polished and eloquent as it may be.

Even if an imposter essay sneaks past admissions and the student is accepted to the college, the student will, for their college years and for the rest of their life, know that they didn't earn their admission on their own merits. They cheated to get in. It can undermine a student's self-confidence and damage the parent/student relationship for years to come.

KEY TAKEAWAYS

1) Most of my clients apply to at least one college that requires a 650-word essay for the Common Application. That's a key essay to finalize over the summer.

2) The student can review the colleges on their list and see which require a "Why Our College?" essay. The student should have their half of the Zipper Technique ready to go and should write at least one of these essays over the summer.

3) Help your student brainstorm stories and incidents from their life that might work as an essay topic. Common prompts ask students to reflect on their community, their impact, their extracurricular activities, and why

they are interested in the major they've indicated in the application.

4) Have someone who knows something about college essays proofread and check the stories for appropriateness of topic, tone, grammar, and punctuation.

13

Application Portals

The application portals are the online sites where the student fills out the application forms and uploads their essays, résumé, and other relevant materials. Some of the most frequently used portals include the Common Application, ApplyTexas, the University of California, and the California State University system portals. Understanding and managing the application portals is key to getting everything pulled together and submitted on time, so students will need to stay on top of the process.

Part of what makes applying to college complicated is that there are so many websites and application portals for students to track, which is one reason it's helpful to keep all the links and login information in one key document or spreadsheet. If your student is unfamiliar with how to use a spreadsheet, now might be a great opportunity for you to help them build that skill.

Most students who are applying to private four-year colleges end up creating accounts at several of the application portals. Students can search the admissions page of each college's website to find out which application portal(s) they use. A few schools, including MIT, Georgetown University, Endicott College, and many art schools, have their own application portals—ones not shared with any other colleges.

All the main portals open up for the fall application season in early August, so it's a good idea to set aside several days or a few weekends in that month for the student to enter the details for each application. This is not difficult work, but it is tedious and time consuming.

Here are the most frequently used portals:

THE COMMON APPLICATION
CommonApp.org

Students can apply to more than 900 colleges via the Common Application. This website shuts down at the end of July each year, purges all the deadlines, essay prompts, and information from the last admission cycle, and then comes back online on or around August 1 for the new admission cycle.

The "common" part of the application (and the only part that is not purged at the end of July) falls under the "Common App" tab on the student account's home page. It includes the student's full legal name, information about parents and siblings, and current or most recent high school (with room to add high schools if the student attended more than one). This core information about the student is sent to all the colleges the student is applying to on the Common App.

The "College Search" tab allows students to select from among all the Common App's 900 colleges and add the colleges on their list to the "My Colleges" tab, which contains school-specific data the student needs to enter for each college. If you'd like to watch a video walk-through of these sections of the Common App, visit this book's resources page at https://www.CollegePrepCounseling.com/resources.

APPLYTEXAS
goapplytexas.org

There are 53 schools in the Lone Star State that use the Apply-Texas application, including Southern Methodist University and the University of Texas campuses at El Paso, Austin, Dallas, and Arlington. The application traditionally opens on August 1 for that fall's admission season.

The ApplyTexas application has three sections. In the first section, the student needs to enter their profile information (name, address, birthday and city/country of birth, high school, etc.). It's a pain, as there are 10 pages to the profile, and you cannot move on until all the information is completed for each page in sequence. In addition, it asks for information that is largely irrelevant to an applicant unless someday they actually end up on campus (i.e., emergency contact information).

In the second section, the student can start an application to a specific Texas school. Note that the ApplyTexas application breaks down activities and extracurriculars into four pages: extracurricular, community/volunteer service, talents/honors/awards, and employment/internships/summer activities. The student should plan ahead how they will divide up their activities to span these different pages.

The third section allows the student to submit the application once it is completed.

THE UNIVERSITY OF CALIFORNIA
apply.universityofcalifornia.edu

There are nine University of California (known as "UC") campuses that accept applications from high school students for freshman admission: UC Berkeley, UC Davis, UC Irvine, UC Los Angeles (known as UCLA), UC Merced, UC Riverside, UC San Diego, UC Santa Barbara, and UC Santa Cruz.

Along with all the other portals we've discussed so far, the UC application opens for students to start filling out the forms on August 1. However, students can only submit completed applications between October 1 and November 30.

The application is the same whether the student is applying to one UC or to all the UCs. The only difference is that the student will need to indicate the major they are interested in and pay the extra $70 application fee for each campus. The application requires that the student write four "Personal Insight Questions" of up to 350 words each, regardless of whether the student is applying to only one campus or to several of the campuses. The eight prompts that students can pick from don't tend to change much from year to year. If you do an internet search on "UC PIQs," you'll be able to find the prompts quickly.

THE CALIFORNIA STATE UNIVERSITY SYSTEM (CSU)
calstate.edu/apply

There are 23 California State University colleges, including CSU Long Beach, CSU Fullerton, San Diego State University, Chico State University, San Jose State University, and the two polytechnic campuses, Cal Poly San Luis Obispo and Cal Poly Pomona.

There is only one application, but each campus the student is applying to will have a few quick questions for the student to answer. There are no essays and they do not ask for letters of recommendation or detailed information about the student's extracurricular activities.

APPLYSUNY
suny.edu/applysuny/

More than 50 of the State University of New York (SUNY) system schools use the applySUNY application portal. There is a base SUNY application and then a supplemental application for some campuses. The application will walk the student through a series of pages, indicated by tabs at the top of the page, asking questions about their name, address, date of birth, family, education, activities, work experiences, etc. Some, but not all, campuses require an essay. They've aligned the SUNY essay prompt and word limit with those of the main Common App essay, so the student ought to be able to reuse their Common App essay here.

ALIGNING THE STUDENT'S ACTIVITIES LIST TO EACH PORTAL

In Chapter 4, I discussed the importance of a student résumé. Once the student has started creating accounts in the various portals, they'll need to take the information from the résumé and repurpose it to fit the activities section of each portal. Many colleges let the student upload their actual résumé, but that is in addition to, not instead of, the activities list.

In the activities section in the Common Application, students are instructed to list their activities *in order of importance* to the student. I also tell students that the order should consider which activities best support the narrative of the application. For example, prospective engineering majors might want to list their engineering accomplishments first. Also note that, in the Common Application portal, the student is limited to only 10 entries.

I like having students start with the résumé because they have free rein to describe in detail what they've done for each activity. Then, in the activities lists in the application portals, they can decide how to condense the information to fit the word or character limits. The application portals have very specific formats that the student must follow to enter their activity details. These formats severely limit the number of words or characters a student can use to describe what they've done.

For example, in the Common App, students are limited to 50 characters to describe their position, 100 characters to describe the organization, and 150 characters to describe what they did. This means students need to be clever and concise regarding how they present the information. Here's how our lacrosse player from the résumé example in Chapter 4 might list that in the Common App:

Activity type: Athletics: JV/Varsity (from the pull-down menu)
Sport/Team: Lacrosse (from the pull-down menu)
Position/Leadership description (maximum characters: 50): Team Captain
Organization Name (maximum characters: 100): Summerville High School Varsity Lacrosse Team
Please describe this activity, including what you accomplished and any recognition you received, etc. (maximum characters: 150):

Organized team meetings; assisted in developing training schedule; helped resolve conflicts/boost morale. Took team to state championships.

I have a video walk-through showing how to complete this section of the Common App on this book's resources page at https://www.CollegePrepCounseling.com/resources.

ACTIVITIES LISTS IN OTHER PORTALS

Your student may be submitting applications using some of the other portals that we've discussed. Each is a bit different and will require that the student once again rearrange their main activities.

For example, in the University of California application, students can list up to 20 activities and use up to 350 characters for each description. As previously mentioned, the ApplyTexas application has different pages for the student to use for different types of activities (Extracurricular Activities, Community/Volunteer Service, Talents/Awards/Honors). The student should preview the activities sections for each of their portals and then adjust the organization of their activities accordingly.

SCHOOL-SPECIFIC PORTALS FOR AFTER THE APPLICATIONS ARE SUBMITTED

After a student has submitted their applications from the various portals, some colleges send applicants to a new, college-specific web portal that allows students to check the status of their application (for example, have all the components been received by the college or is something missing?), communicate about deadlines, and deliver final admissions and financial aid decisions.

It's critical that students keep track of the URL and their personal login information for each of these portals. They should log in regularly to ensure that their application is complete and that they answer any additional questions the colleges might have.

Be aware that it can sometimes take several days for colleges to gather and consolidate the documents that are sent from the student, from the high school, and from the testing agencies, and then a bit longer to update the portal information. If your student is certain that everything has been sent, do not panic if they get a message saying their application is incomplete. Have them check in with their high school counselor if they feel there may have been a delay or error. More often than not, giving the portal a few days to update will resolve any issues.

KEY TAKEAWAYS

1) Help your student tease out which application portal they'll need for each college on the student's list. If possible, find ways to minimize the number of portals the student needs to use.

2) Have your student set aside time in early August to do the necessary but tedious task of filling in all the data that the application portals request of them.

3) Ensure they are keeping all the links to each of their portals, plus their usernames and passwords, in a key document that is readily accessible and not easily lost.

4) Have them preview the different formats for the activities lists in each of their portals (Common App,

ApplyTexas, University of California, etc.) once the portals open up in August before their senior year.

5) Make sure their activities are listed in the order of importance to the student's application.

6) Remember to have the student look for an email from the colleges after they've submitted the application. There will probably be one about setting up their college-specific portal.

14

Early Decision and Other Admissions Options

S tudents can submit their applications using a variety of admissions options that can sometimes be confusing. There is a lot of gamesmanship involved in deciding the best course of action for a student as they consider how to apply to a school. It would be very helpful for you to be able to help your student think this through strategically, so it's important that you and your student understand what these options are and how they can affect your student's chances of getting admitted.

When I work with students, we spend a lot of time going through the pros and cons of various application strategies for different schools. My goal is to make sure they understand all their options and the repercussions of their choices so they can make informed decisions throughout the process.

The most common admission options are listed below, but keep in mind that colleges don't normally offer *all* these options. Each college offers its own mix-and-match menu, so your student will need to find out the specifics for the colleges on their list.

EARLY DECISION

Early Decision is the 800-pound gorilla among the admissions options because an Early Decision application is binding—that is, if a student is admitted under the Early Decision program, then they *must* enroll at that school (caveat below). That means students should only apply to a college via Early Decision if it is definitely their first-choice college.

Early Decision is an option mainly offered by private colleges. Many colleges that offer Early Decision fill a good portion of their incoming freshman class with Early Decision candidates. For example, for the Class of 2024 (high school students who graduated in 2020), Middlebury College filled 65% of its class from its Early Decision applicant pool; Pitzer College, 79.5%; Emory University, 59.8%; Cornell University, 49.1%; Tulane University, 51.2%. Now you know why it's so important, from a strategic perspective, to consider having your student apply Early Decision if their first-choice school is one that fills most of the class from this pool of candidates.

Depending on the college, Early Decision candidates can have about the same percent chance of admission as Regular Decision candidates (which washes away any strategic advantage for applying under this binding option) or it can give them a boost of two, three, or almost four times the likelihood of getting admitted. For example, at Haverford College, Class of

2024, 46.1% of Early Decision candidates were accepted, while only 15.3% of Regular Decision candidates were admitted. At Northwestern, 25.1% of Early Decision applicants were accepted while only 7.3% of Regular Decision candidates were. For a link to a list of colleges and their Early Decision admission rates, visit this book's resources page at https://www. CollegePrepCounseling.com/resources.

As the name implies, Early Decision applications are due early, usually by November 1 or November 15, depending on the college. That's about eight weeks earlier than the Regular Decision application deadlines, which usually fall around January 1 or January 15.

However, more recently, some colleges have begun to offer "Early Decision, Round 2" (often shortened to ED II). Basically, this is still a binding decision, but the application is due on or close to the deadline for the Regular Decision candidates (so not really early at all anymore, but still binding). The ED II option can be used by students who didn't have their application ready to go for a college in time to meet the Early Decision, Round 1 (ED I) deadline. It can also be used by students who applied to their first-choice school ED I and were denied admission or deferred (that is, no decision was made, and the college moved that applicant to the Regular Decision pool, thus releasing that student from the Early Decision commitment).

Here's the Early Decision caveat: ED is intended to be binding, but students can wriggle out of it if the college does not offer sufficient financial aid to make it affordable for the family, and what is "affordable" to the family is determined by ... the family. That said, families should run through the net cost calculator for the college before applying Early Decision so that they know if the college is, financially, a realistic option for the student.

A student can apply to only one school in the first round of Early Decision and only one school in the second round (and they can only apply to an ED II school if they did not get admitted to the first ED school or did not apply to a first-round ED school). For any Early Decision application, both you (the parent) and the school counselor need to sign off on special forms to acknowledge that the student is signing a binding agreement.

If a student applies Early Decision, they can hear one of three results from the college:

1) Admitted—yay! The student is in. Time to celebrate (and look carefully at the financial aid offer).
2) Denied—boo! Time to grieve and process that loss for a few days, and then have the student pick themselves up and move on to the next college (easier said than done, I know).
3) Deferred—that means that the college didn't make a final decision one way or the other. We'll talk about how to deal with that in Chapter 17, "What to Do Once Decisions Come Out."

─────────── **Pro Tip** ───────────

Even if your student applies Early Decision to a college, encourage them to continue to finish application essays for the other schools on their list. There is only a short window of time—about two weeks—between when the Early Decision notifications are sent (usually in mid-December) and when the Regular Decision applications are due. If the student does *not* get admitted to their ED I college, more than likely they will feel deflated for at least a few days and not in the mood to write more college essays. (And if they do have to write those essays, they'll be feeling less confident and perhaps a bit desperate—which is not a good frame of mind for essay writing.) So, get those essays written before the Early Decision results come out.

EARLY ACTION

Unlike Early Decision, the Early Action option is not binding. Early Action (EA) allows students who have their applications done early to submit them to colleges and get decisions back in mid-December or in January, rather than having to wait until late March or early April to get an admissions decision. The admission offers aren't binding, so students still have until the traditional May 1 deadline to decide where to enroll.

Unfortunately, more and more colleges seem to be deferring EA students to the Regular Decision round (described below) rather than make a firm yes-or-no decision in the early round. Some are even nudging the students to switch their EA application to ED II. Why? The colleges want the student to commit. They don't want to "waste" an offer of admission on a student who might not actually enroll in their college (thus lowering their "yield" numbers).

Some colleges don't offer Early Decision but do offer Early Action. Others offer both ED and EA. I mentioned earlier that most public colleges do not offer Early Decision, but a few do offer Early Action.

Strategically, the dilemma can come for a student whose first-choice school does not offer Early Decision. One of my students loved the University of Michigan—it was by far her number one choice. As a public college, they offered Early Action but not Early Decision. Unfortunately, even for the Early Action students, they do not give admissions decisions until the end of January. That meant that my student, for whom UMich was a real reach based on her GPA—meaning she was not likely to be offered admission—was not able to apply to any school Early Decision, as she wanted to be able to attend UMich if they indeed offered her a spot. If UMich had announced their EA decision in mid-December, my student could have selected another school for the ED II round. So, her love of UMich meant that she wasn't eligible for a potential ED boost at her second- or third-choice schools, which may mean she won't end up at any of her top three choices (then again, she's already been admitted to a few other schools on her list, so we know she'll have a good option one way or another).

RESTRICTIVE EARLY ACTION

Stanford, Notre Dame, Georgetown, and Harvard are a few of the colleges that offer Early Action but no Early Decision. But there's a catch. Each of these schools has a bit of a different spin on what's allowed and what's not. They call it "Restrictive Early Action" or "Single-Choice Early Action," and it's crucial to read the fine print of what is and is not acceptable in terms of where else the student can and cannot apply under these rules.

Here's an example of how this can get complicated. At Stanford, if you apply via Restrictive Early Action, you may not apply Early Decision or Early Action to any other private colleges, nor can you apply to any public university's options that are binding.

At Notre Dame, their Restrictive Early Action program allows students to apply to other colleges EA but restricts students from applying to other colleges via Early Decision. Georgetown's Early Action program follows the same rules (that is, it's okay to apply elsewhere EA but not ED), but they never deny students in the Early Action round. Students are either admitted or deferred to the Regular Decision round. In addition, students admitted via EA may not then apply to another college via ED II.

Harvard has a Restrictive Early Action program. Students are permitted to apply early to public or foreign colleges, as long as those applications are not binding if the student is admitted. In addition, Harvard REA applicants may not apply EA to other private U.S. colleges or universities. However, applicants may apply ED II to another school after they've received their admissions decision from Harvard. Here's another twist, though: students may not apply to another private school that has an "early consideration" involved—for example, the student would not be allowed to apply to USC by their December 1 priority deadline for merit scholarship consideration.

As you can see, this can get tricky! My team and I spend a lot of time with our individual and group-session clients teasing this out to ensure each student is following all the rules with their admissions strategy. And, as mentioned earlier, it's critical that your student understands the difference between public and private colleges when figuring out what is and is not allowed.

REGULAR DECISION

Regular Decision is the bread-and-butter application option. The student applies in the standard time frame, not early. Most

Regular Decision deadlines fall around either November 30 or January 1. The Regular Decision option is not binding, but also doesn't have a strategic advantage. Regular Decision admission announcements are usually made in late March or early April.

One thing you may want to emphasize with your student is that, while they can sometimes turn in a homework assignment a day or so late and still get credit, that is *not* the case with college admissions. If the student misses the deadline, even by a few seconds, they aren't applying that year. End of story. Done. Not applying. These are rock solid deadlines that do not have one iota of wiggle room.

Don't believe me? This year, I had a student applying to Williams College via Early Decision. The ED deadline was November 15 at midnight. Luckily, the Williams application was one of those that lets the student submit the main part of the application in one section and the optional writing supplement in another section. On November 15th—deadline day!—he sent in the main part of his application. But then he decided to take one more look at his writing supplement before submitting the second part. He pushed the button on the supplement at 11:59 p.m., thinking he'd slide in just before the deadline. Nope. There was one more screen that asked him to review the PDF and confirm that the supplement read like he wanted it to. That slight delay meant he submitted the optional writing supplement 17 seconds late—and it was blocked. They would not accept it. The deadline had passed. Thank goodness that essay was optional and not required.

So, he had applied on time, but did not get the boost he would have gotten if he'd been able to include that paper as part of his application. (As it turns out, his main essay, GPA, test scores, and activities were outstanding, and he got in anyway—phew!) And quick note—I always encourage students to submit their applications at least a week before the deadlines to avoid this kind of situation and to minimize the stress.

ROLLING ADMISSIONS

Schools that offer Rolling Admissions "roll" with the applications as they come in. They review an application soon after it is submitted and deliver a decision within a few weeks. I love rolling admissions schools! These schools tend to offer admission to the majority of students who apply, so my students who apply to rolling schools (as early as August before senior year starts) can often get an offer of admission early in their senior year, relieving the stress they may feel wondering if any college will offer them a place. Having a college acceptance in their pockets early builds their confidence for the rest of the process.

Popular schools that offer rolling admissions include Arizona State University and University of Arizona, Indiana University (Bloomington), and several of the California State universities (including CSU Long Beach, CSU Northridge, and Cal Poly Pomona).

PRIORITY ADMISSIONS

Priority applications can mean different things at different colleges, but, generally, this has to do with getting an application in earlier than the Regular Decision deadline in order to be considered for maximum financial aid and scholarship consideration. At USC, for example, students who submit their applications by the priority deadline (historically, December 1) will be considered for merit scholarships. Students not interested in merit scholarships can wait until the Regular Decision deadline in January to submit their applications.

KEY TAKEAWAYS

1) Make sure you and your student understand the meaning of terms such as Early Decision, Early Action, Restrictive Early Action, Rolling Admission, etc.
2) Understand the strategic pros and cons of each type of application.
3) Determine with the student how and when they will apply to each college on their list.

15

Interviews

College admissions interviews can be a source of huge stress for students. They imagine that these interviews carry as much weight as, say, a job interview. But, in my experience, that's not the case at all. Most interviews are conducted by the colleges' alumni, and even if the alum finds the student to be fascinating and amazing and wonderful, it often doesn't count a whole lot in terms of helping the student get admitted. Several of my friends, including alums from Stanford and Harvard, bemoan the fact that they've interviewed many incredible students whom they have enthusiastically endorsed, only for that student to be denied admission anyway. (Cynical observation: colleges use their alums to do interviews as a way of keeping the alum connected to the college—and therefore continuing to make donations—so it really isn't *only* about the search for the best students.)

On the flip side, the interviews really can't hurt the applicant unless the student is profoundly uncomfortable in social situations and makes the situation painful for both themselves and the interviewer. Several of my autism-spectrum clients would fall into this category because they find that these types of social situations trigger their anxiety. For those students, I often recommend that they just skip the interview if it is optional. But most of the students I work with in either my group or individual sessions are articulate and have lots to say once they get comfortable. Let them know it's okay to have fun in the interview conversation!

PREPARATION

If your student does choose to interview, there are a few key ways to prepare. In general, students who think they might be interviewing for colleges (or future jobs!) should take the opportunity months or years beforehand to put down their cell phones and talk to adults in their everyday world. A key factor in the interviews is whether the student can carry on an interesting conversation with someone they've just met, and keep it going for 20 to 60 minutes. There's no better way to prepare than to have had a whole lot of conversational practice with adults—basically, anyone over the age of their peers, but even better if it's someone over 35. A great opener for those in middle school or early high school? The student can tell the person they are speaking with that they are thinking of going to college and then ask whether that person went (and if so, what they thought of their experience). This allows students to gather insights from those who've had a college experience, and it will help the student get comfortable asking questions and engaging in dialogue.

When it comes time for the actual college admissions interview, the student should be prepared to talk about themselves—who they are, how they came to have their current values and goals, and where they are headed—with confidence but without arrogance. It helps if the student has a mental inventory of short stories or anecdotes to tell that relay their interest in an academic or extracurricular activity. Stories are more memorable for the interviewer and can help enliven the conversation. A few stories to have on hand (and which could very well come from the student's essays, which the interviewer likely will not have had access to):

- A time when the student faced and overcame a challenge
- An anecdote showing persistence and work ethic
- A story that demonstrates integrity or honesty
- A vision for how they'd be active on campus
- The story of how they decided on a specific major

Students may need a reminder that the college interview is not an interrogation, with the interviewer sitting on one side of the desk peppering the student with a list of questions. It really is much more of a back-and-forth conversation. In fact, asking a question of the interviewer (a question that gets the interviewer talking about themselves) can be very helpful to give the student a break to gather their thoughts and take a breath in the middle of the interview. If the interviewer is an alum of the college, what did they like best about their time there? Why did they choose that college over any others they were considering? Is there anything they would have done differently regarding their college careers?

If an interviewer asks a question that really stumps the student, the student should not be afraid to say, "Let me think about that for a minute." There is no need to rush into an answer. Pausing to consider shows that the student is taking the time to weigh their words and think up a response rather than blurting out a quick answer.

Alum interviewers may not have any formal training in how to conduct an interview, but most conscientious alums will understand that students get nervous, so the alum may be looking for ways to make the student feel at ease and comfortable. So let them know they can relax!

Pro Tip

You can Google the name of your interviewer or search for them on LinkedIn to read a bit more about their background and interests. Although they will likely see that you have done so, it shows you're paying attention and doing due diligence in your research. After coaching one of my students to prepare her for a University of Pennsylvania (Wharton) interview, we discovered her interviewer was very interested in poker and the statistical probabilities around that game. My student found a clever way to mention an aspect of poker in her interview, and the interviewer eagerly jumped in to chat about that topic, extending their discussion by another 20 minutes.

KNOW THE COLLEGE

Students should be very familiar with the college before that college's interview—what it offers and specific reasons why that school is a great fit for them. They should be able to discuss potential majors and what their possible plans are after they graduate.

Earlier in the book, we discussed the importance of taking detailed notes on each college when doing research. This is the time to pull out that research, especially the notes on "why this college?" and review them before the interview.

I happen to have a copy of an Ivy League college's interview form that they distribute to their alum interviewers. The interviewers are asked, basically, to relay the conversation to the admissions committee:

- Did the student describe any favorite activities or classes?
- What were some of their experiences that made the biggest impact on them?
- Were they able to articulate why they want to attend this particular college—any unique programs or resources they'd like to incorporate into their undergraduate years?

ZOOM ETIQUETTE

If the student's interview will be conducted virtually, they should take the time to ensure that their background is presentable—no unmade beds, no underwear hanging out of an open dresser drawer, no questionable posters on the wall. And certainly no pennants from other colleges! They should show the interviewer that they took some care and had the foresight to clean up. Make sure the lighting is good and that the student's face is not darkened as if they were in a witness protection program. If there are loud siblings or barking dogs in the house, you, as the parent, can pile everyone except the interviewee into the minivan and go grab an ice cream during the interview so the student doesn't have to worry about embarrassing interruptions.

CLEARING CRUTCH WORDS

If the interviewer is over the age of 35, the student would be wise to practice clearing any crutch words before the interview. To be more specific: students who have the habit of peppering the word "like" throughout their speech should practice turning it off before they get to the interview, as it can be not only distracting but downright irritating for interviewers.

I was once touring a small college in Los Angeles (regularly touring colleges keeps me updated on what's happening at different campuses), and, for 90 minutes, I had to listen to the student tour guide use the word "like" for every other word. "This is, like, the biology building, and, like, this is, like, the cafeteria." It was a wonderful college, but the main thing I remember about that tour—even this many years later—is the tour guide and her "like" habit. So please gently encourage your student to check their own speech if they have this habit or any other speech tics such as "um" or "y'know."

SEND A THANK YOU

A day or two after the interview, I check in with my clients to make sure they've sent the interviewer a quick thank-you note, either by email or even snail mail, to thank them for taking the time to meet.

KEY TAKEAWAYS

1) Try to help the student relax. The interviews are among the least important factors in the application process.

2) Find opportunities for your teen to interact with your friends as an authentic way to practice their socialization and conversation skills.

3) As with brainstorming essay topics, help the student come up with short stories to share that demonstrate their persistence, work ethic, or other characteristics that make them well-suited to a challenging college environment.

4) Make sure the student is familiar with the college and can articulate why that college is such a great fit for them.

5) Gently bring to their attention any overuse of crutch words so they build their awareness and can weed them out as much as possible before the interview.

6) Encourage your student to send a thank-you note a day or so after the interview.

16

Special Supplements for Art, Dance, Drama, and Music

If your student has a special talent in dance, music, painting, photography, or another art form, most colleges will allow them to showcase their accomplishments in a special supplement to the main application. This can be a great way for the student to show off a talent that sets them apart from the main pool of applicants. I'm not talking here about students who are auditioning for a spot as a music, theater, or dance major, or applying to an art school via a portfolio—those are special applications and auditions that are beyond the scope of this book. However, for students who don't necessarily want to major in those areas, but still have talent they'd like to showcase to the admissions committee, it can add an extra dimension of depth to the application.

One of my students, a young man from a private East Coast high school, wasn't sure what he wanted to study in college, but he submitted an art portfolio as part of his Early Decision application simply to offer the college another point of information about his background. Although his 3.3 GPA was significantly lower than most students admitted to that particular college, he was admitted. We'll never know for sure, but we felt that his artistic talents, as demonstrated in his art portfolio, helped him make his case.

Generally, submitting a portfolio involves having the student collect digital representations of their best work as digital images, videos, or audio files to present to the colleges. These digital portfolios are considered supplemental materials and are handled outside of the standard application portal, usually uploaded to a third-party website (SlideRoom.com is the most common) that is set up to handle these types of materials.

Colleges using SlideRoom will have their own SlideRoom.com accounts (for example, Denison University SlideRoom account is located at denison.slideroom.com). Colleges give detailed instructions about what to include in the portfolio either in the main application or on the supplement page itself.

Be sure your student reads each college's portfolio instructions carefully. Colleges, especially colleges of art and design, are very specific about the types, sizes, and contents of materials the portfolio should include. For example, the Rhode Island School of Design (RISD) has for years required that art students submit a drawing of a bicycle (Google "RISD bicycle" and you'll see some fun examples). Some colleges expect to receive these supplemental materials by the submission deadline. Others give a bit of leeway in the timing of submitting the supplements. Students need to read carefully or call the school admissions department to find out when the portfolio is due.

Watch out, though! Students may not be able to access a college's SlideRoom (or another portal) until after they've submitted their main application and the school has, in turn, sent the applicant access to the college's applicant portal … and that can take a few days. If the student submits their Common Application on the deadline day, they will not necessarily get access to the portal in time to upload the supplementary material.

I advise any students who plan to submit supplementary materials to make sure they submit their main application at least two weeks *prior to* the deadline so that they have time to get their supplementary materials submitted by the actual deadline.

Also, families should be aware that there is often an extra fee ($5 or more) that the applicant must pay to include these supplementary materials in the application. Those are paid at the SlideRoom site.

Students who are submitting applications to a university or college's school of music, dance, or theater should confirm the application deadlines, which can be earlier than the school's deadline for other applicants.

KEY TAKEAWAYS

1) Art, music, dance, and photography portfolios can add another dimension to a student's application.
2) These require extra planning and preparation on the part of the student but can enhance an application and help the student stand out from the crowd.

17

What to Do Once Decisions Come Out

The applications are submitted, and the student finally gets to take a deep breath because they're done ... right? Absolutely take the time to appreciate this accomplishment. With your support, your student has put in time and effort doing research, entering data into forms, writing essays, and gathering letters of recommendation. There's much to celebrate! But they aren't done yet. They'll still need to check the portals for news and strategize how to move forward when they are deferred, accepted, or waitlisted.

CHECK THE PORTALS

A few days after the student has submitted an application, they should check the college portal to ensure that the college has received all the application materials that have been sent. It can take a few days for everything to work through the system and be acknowledged, so keep monitoring it, but have some patience if things don't appear right away.

DEFERRED

A deferral happens when a student who applied Early Action or Early Decision is not given a clear "yes, we're offering you admission" or "no, we're sorry, but we do not have room for you" answer. A deferral means that a decision has not yet been made, and the application has been moved to the Regular Decision round. For Early Decision applications, this then releases the student from the binding agreement. The student is free to apply to another school for Early Decision, Round II in addition to all their other Regular Decision schools. If they are later admitted to the original ED college in the Regular Decision round, they can accept the offer (unless their ED II school admits them, which is binding), but they are not obligated to do so.

If your student is deferred, have them check their portal for that college to see if there are instructions for sending a Letter of Continued Interest to let the college know the student would still like to be considered for admission. If there are no explicit instructions, have your student send an email to that college's admissions representative reiterating their continued interest in that college and providing a short update on any new activities or accomplishments since the original application was sent.

WAITLISTED

Waitlisting happens after decisions are made in the Regular Decision round. The student was not offered admission but was put on the waitlist in case spots open up later. Follow the college's instructions—do they want the student to let them know whether they want to stay on the waitlist? If your student does want to stay on the waitlist, let the college know by following whatever instructions the college sends.

The student should check the Common Data Set for the college to see how many students they put on the waitlist last year, and, of those, how many were eventually offered admission.

Meanwhile, your student will still need to put down a deposit at another school by the May 1 deadline, and if they get off the waitlist after May 1 and want to switch their enrollment, they'll lose their deposit at the first school.

ACCEPTED!

Whoo-hoo, time to celebrate your student and their accomplishments, not only in the admissions process but in all the years leading up to this moment. Time for the parents to celebrate, too. It's a major accomplishment to raise a child and launch them into adulthood via the road through college. Congratulations!

ACCEPTED ... BUT WITH AN INSUFFICIENT FINANCIAL AID PACKAGE

What if your student has several offers of admission, but the financial aid package offered by their top-choice college falls short of what your family can afford? You can appeal the *need-based* portion of a financial aid offer if you have documentation of special circumstances that aren't reflected in your FAFSA® (remember, the income information you reported is a few years old and may no longer accurately reflect your family's situation).

You can also request additional *merit* aid from one college if a similar college (in terms of size and selectivity) offered your student more merit money, letting the first college know that your student will enroll if they can match the other college's offer. For detailed information on this topic, I recommend financial aid guru Mark Kantrowitz's book, *How to Appeal for More College Financial Aid.*

WARN YOUR STUDENT ABOUT SENIORITIS

College applications, homecoming, and senior year courses can leave students exhausted after winter break. But let the students know that they need to maintain their grades through graduation. A drop in grades below their normal threshold can lead to a college revoking its offer of admission, and if that happens in late June or in July, the student will be scrambling to find another college before the fall semester.

NATIONAL COLLEGE DECISION DAY – MAY 1

Last year, one of my brightest students was admitted to all 12 colleges to which he applied. We were very strategic about his application. We got his essays done early (by "we" here, I mean that he wrote them, and we gave feedback and did a final proofread) and he was able to submit the majority of his applications Early Action. He knew by mid-December that he had a lot of offers on the table. He didn't have a favorite college, and he was applying to colleges where his grades and test scores were way above the averages for admitted students, so there was no reason to apply anywhere Early Decision.

With 12 offers on the table, he now needed to choose where he would enroll, and he needed to let the college know by the

National College Decision date of May 1. That's the traditional date that students need to make a commitment to one college among those that offer them admission.

For this student, his family did not qualify for need-based aid, but because he was such a stellar candidate (and because we had crafted his college list wisely), his colleges offered him considerable merit money. He ended up picking the college that offered him $220,000 over four years, or $55,000 per year, bringing the cost of that college down to the equivalent of going to an in-state college. He was thrilled, his parents were thrilled, and I was thrilled! He submitted his enrollment commitment to that school by the May 1 deadline.

Students must make a decision about which college to enroll in by May 1. If they hear back from their colleges by late March or early April, that means the family only has a few weeks to compare financial aid offers, make final visits to the colleges where they've been offered admission (the victory tour), and picture themselves packing up and moving to their new home.

This is also the time to visit any reach or lottery schools if the student was admitted. Now the student can go knowing that they are *in* and it really is an option for them. But don't forget to follow the college's procedures to commit to their college of choice by the May 1 deadline. Missing the deadline indirectly tells the college that your student does not intend to enroll, giving the college the option to offer that spot to a student on its waiting list.

KEY TAKEAWAYS

1) It's imperative that students check their application portals regularly.

2) Students who are deferred should send a Letter of Continued Interest to the college.

3) Students who are waitlisted should check the Common Data Set to get some idea of how likely it will be that they are offered a spot.

4) The student needs to make their final choice and put down a deposit by the enrollment deadline, which is usually May 1.

18

If You'd Like More Help

My goal with this book has been to give you plenty of clear information and pro tips to help you support your student and keep you both sane through the college application process.

But if, after reading this, you feel as though this admissions project is more than you'd like to tackle alone, or if you'd like a deeper level of support and guidance, please know that we are here to help. We've been through this process, and we know how to work with students to get them across the finish line. If you want to take a deep breath, lift this weight off your shoulders, and hand off the niggly details, accountability check-ins, and the occasional necessary nudging, reach out. My team and I offer online classes, small group sessions, one-to-one counseling, essay editing and proofing, application audits, and more to help every family get precisely the support and guidance they need. You can find us at CollegePrepCounseling.com. We work through the summer (especially during the summer!) and offer evening and weekend hours so we can work with students on their schedules and keep things moving when school counseling offices are closed.

You can also ask me questions and keep informed by joining the book's Facebook group at https://www.facebook.com/groups/admissionessentials.

I have a wish for you and your student for this application process. For you, I hope it brings pride in the amazing young person you have helped raise and a sense of knowing you did everything you could to give them the best guidance possible along the way. For your child, I hope it brings clarity in defining who they are, what they want out of college and for their future, and a system to tackle the applications in a less stressful and more sane way. May your child be admitted to all the colleges that would be their perfect match.

WHAT PARENTS SAY ABOUT WORKING WITH BETH

"We were late preparing for SAT and college applications. Hiring Beth allowed my daughter to prioritize what needed to be done over the summer and have a solid plan for her senior fall semester. She felt supported and understood the process and Beth was available to help along the way."

"Working with College Prep Counseling reduced my stress level since I knew the process and deadlines were being managed by a pro. This in turn made the household more peaceful."

"My student is an extremely reluctant applicant. Having Beth engaged in the process helped reduce the overall stress level."

"The process seemed to us as parents of an athlete and not the most highly motivated student, absolutely daunting. To be able to place 100% trust and faith in a knowledgeable professional who truly cares about her students was a gift we cannot begin to place a value on. The 'household dynamic' was stressed enough over the process of trying to get recruited during the year of COVID. Beth gently guiding our son and alleviating us of the responsibility I'm certain spared us much stress and heartache."

"It would have been extremely difficult to navigate this process without knowledgeable assistance. Beth held our son's hand every step of the way until the last application was submitted."

"All our questions and concerns were always fully addressed in a timely manner. Beth is a very caring professional."

Note: Names have been omitted from the quotes to ensure client confidentiality.

About the Author

B eth Pickett is the founder of College Prep Counseling. She has been working with students across the U.S. as a college admissions counselor for more than a decade. Her clients and essay students have earned admission to Harvard, Yale, Brown, UC Berkeley, UCLA, Stanford, Williams, UMich, Tulane, Colgate, Cornell, Lewis & Clark, Hamilton, and many other colleges and universities across the U.S.

A graduate of Stanford, Beth studied human and marine biology in college. She completed a post-graduate year afield, joining underwater expeditions with the National Geographic Society and the Cousteau Society.

She went on to earn her Certificate in College Counseling from UCLA and launched College Prep Counseling in 2007. She started teaching summer essay-writing seminars to more than 80 rising seniors annually and then leading a team of editors to review the essays and offer suggestions for improvements before they were submitted to the colleges.

College Prep Counseling has expanded over the years to include not only one-to-one counseling for individual students, but the *3-2-1 Launch!* live online program for groups of up to six students, supporting students who don't like to be in the one-to-one spotlight (and decreasing the costs for the families). College Prep Counseling also offers independent-study online courses to help guide students and their families through the application process, organizing, and pacing their progress so they meet the submission deadlines without stress.

Beth has worked with students from many public and private high schools across the U.S., including St. Paul's (NH), Saint Ann's (NY), Horace Mann (NY), Dalton (NY), Fordham Prep (NY), Ethical Culture Fieldston (NY), Thacher (CA), Academy of Science (VA), Torrey Pines (CA), St. Mary (MI), Acalanes (CA), Portledge (NY), La Salle College High (PA), Villanova Prep (CA), Phoenix Country Day (AZ), Xavier College Preparatory (AZ), and Foothill Tech (CA).

Her philosophy of college admissions is founded on the principle that students who dig deeply into their interests during high school become happier, more accomplished students who are able to submit more compelling college applications. By developing the ability to articulate their goals, students learn about themselves and how to make a plan to move forward in a methodical and precise way. She feels privileged to guide families and mentor students as they navigate the rite of passage that is selective college admissions.

Beth is a member of the Higher Education Consultants Association (HECA) and resides in the seaside town of Ventura, California.

Month-by-Month To-Do List for Students

Below you'll find a monthly checklist of items to complete starting in the summer before junior year begins. If you are starting later than that, just do the best you can to tackle those earlier tasks in the time frame you have left before applications are due.

August before junior year:

- Print and post prominently the Common App grid that teachers use when filling out their letters of recommendation. Students should adjust how they present themselves in class with these criteria in mind. (Visit https://www.CollegePrepCounseling.com/resources to get the most current link.)

- Set up a for-college-applications-only email address and share the address and login information with your parents.
- Take a diagnostic ACT® assessment and a diagnostic SAT® exam close together to determine which suits you better. Start test prep for that *one* type of test.
- Start crafting your résumé. Continue to add to it as junior year unfolds.
- Stay active in extracurricular activities and try to secure one or two leadership positions. If you have not been involved in extracurricular activities, it's time to sign up!

September of junior year:

- A week or two after school starts, make it a point to introduce yourself to your guidance counselor. This person will be writing you a letter of recommendation for college, and it will help immensely if they actually get to know you first.
- Junior year grades are critical. If you find yourself struggling in any of your classes, utilize your teacher's office hours to get extra help.
- Start thinking about what college factors are important to you. What size of college (in regard to student population)? What type of location (city, rural, suburb)? (Chapter 1)
- Visit easy-to-access nearby colleges to get a baseline understanding of how colleges differ.
- Nurture relationships with teachers because your junior year teachers are usually your best source of strong letters of recommendation. (Chapter 8)

December of junior year:

- Decide whether you'll be taking ACT® or SAT® tests, and if so, when to do testing (March/April/May/June). Then register for those tests. If applying to very selective colleges, plan to take the test more than once to earn a higher superscore, but try to finish your testing before senior year starts.
- Spend time over winter break visiting college websites. Keep notes of what you like and don't like about each college.
- The financial aid clock stops (in terms of the calendar year for which parents will report their income on financial aid forms) on December 31.

January/February of junior year:

- Get familiar with the main Common App essay prompts and begin thinking about the topic you'd like to write about.
- Calculate your academic GPA (that is, your GPA minus grades in PE, health, and other non-academic classes). This GPA is a key component to determine whether a college is a reach, target, or likely school.
- Continue researching colleges. Categorize them into likely, target, reach, and "lottery" schools.
- Update your résumé.
- Meet with your school counselor to keep them updated on your college search. Find out if there is a brag packet or other set of forms you'll need to fill out for letters of recommendation.

- Find out whether your school uses an online system such as Naviance or SCOIR to track college applications. Record your username and password and then explore the system so you know how to use it and can take full advantage of what it offers.
- Map out your senior year coursework. Strive to take the most rigorous classes you can handle, and ensure you've covered all the science, math, English, and social science courses required for the colleges on your list.
- Make plans for summer. Take a course in a subject of interest. Deepen your involvement in an extracurricular or personal project. Plan to write as many college application essays as you can. Set aside time in August for application data entry.

March/April of junior year:

- Begin touring target and likely colleges. (Chapter 10)
- Create an account on the Common App and start entering basic data such as your full legal name, address, school, etc. (Chapter 13)
- Continue researching colleges online.
- Sit for the SAT® or ACT® exam if registered this month.
- If colleges on your list are sending representatives to your high school for a visit, sign up and introduce yourself to the rep.

May of junior year:

- Decide which teachers to ask to write your letters of recommendation and ask before school gets out. Provide the teachers with supporting materials such as your résumé. (Chapters 4 and 8)

- Take AP® or IB® exams. Sit for the SAT® or ACT® exam if registered this month.
- Focus on grades!

June of junior year:

- Finalize your list of colleges, making sure there is a balance among likely, target, reach, and lottery schools.
- Run your college list past your school counselor before school lets out for summer.
- Gather the Common Data Set "C7" chart for each of the colleges on your list, and add those to your college research files.
- Begin drafting your main Common App essay.
- Continue researching colleges online and visiting where possible (if students are on campus).
- Begin working on demonstrated interest for the colleges on your list that track this metric. (Chapter 9)

July after junior year:

- Finalize your main Common App essay.
- Gather a preliminary list of essays you'll need to write for each college on your list, based on the essay prompts those colleges used the prior year. Begin writing. (Chapter 12)
- Continue working on demonstrated interest for the colleges on your list that track this metric. (Chapter 9)

August after junior year:

- The Common App will open on or about August 1 for the new application season. Load your list of colleges and fill out the basic data requested by each college.

- Gather every updated essay prompt from the colleges to which you will apply and compare it to the list you made based on last year's prompts. Note any changes, omissions, or additions. Remember to write down the maximum word count for each essay.
- Note which colleges require a "Why Our College?" essay. These must include specific details unique to each college. They cannot be reused from one school to the next. (Chapter 12)
- Determine which schools, if any, you'll apply to Early Action and/or Early Decision. (Chapter 14)
- Organize the colleges in an application tracking spreadsheet by the final application due date for each college. Work on completing those applications that are due first.
- Keep writing essays. Aim to have most of your essays written *before senior year begins*. (Chapter 11)
- Update and finalize your résumé. Print it to PDF (so it will upload to the application sites properly) and name it in the following file format: "Firstname Lastname Resume.pdf." (Chapter 4)
- Look up the SAT® or ACT® score ranges for the colleges on your list. If your scores are at or above the 50th percentile for students admitted to the college, submit your scores. If your scores are below the 50th percentile for students admitted to that college, you may decide to not submit test scores to that school. (Chapter 6)
- Continue working on demonstrated interest for the colleges on your list that track this metric. (Chapter 9)

September of senior year:

- Check in with each teacher whom you have asked to write a letter of recommendation (or, if you didn't ask at the end of junior year, ask now). (Chapter 8)
- Check in with your school counselor regarding your final college list and the deadlines for your earliest applications. (Chapter 7)
- Check whether any of your college applications are due in mid-October. If so, complete any work necessary to hit those deadlines.
- Continue working on demonstrated interest for the colleges on your list that track this metric.

October of senior year:

- The FAFSA® and CSS Financial Aid Profile® open; have your parent or guardian fill out those forms. (Chapter 2)
- Look up which of your colleges will accept self-reported test scores and which require official test scores to be sent from the College Board (for the SAT® test) or ACT.org (for the ACT® exam). Send the official scores to those colleges that require them (and for which you've decided to submit scores).
- Continue working on demonstrated interest for the colleges on your list that track this metric.
- Submit any applications that are due. Submit them at least a day or two before the deadline!

November of senior year:

- November 1 is the Early Decision and Early Action due date for a number of colleges. Be sure to submit well before the posted deadline.
- Continue working on demonstrated interest for the colleges on your list that track this metric.
- Finish any essays that still need to be written.

December of senior year:

- Submit any applications with early January deadlines *before* school closes for winter break.
- After you send an application, check your college portal to confirm that no components of your application are missing. (Chapter 13)

January of senior year:

- Continue to check your portals.
- Submit any last applications that have mid-January or early February due dates.
- Write and send a "letter of continued interest" if you are deferred from any of your Early Action or Early Decision schools. (Chapter 17)

February of senior year:

- Practice self-care while waiting for decisions. Go for a walk. Play with your dog. Do something fun with a friend or a parent (because in another few months, you won't be living under the same roof with them, and you might actually miss them).

March of senior year:

- Offers start to come in. Do not make any final decisions or commitments until you've heard from all your colleges and/or looked very carefully at each college's financial aid offer.

April of senior year:

- Where possible, plan a tour of the colleges that accepted you to help you make a final decision of where to enroll.
- Make sure to keep your grades up so that you don't risk having your chosen college revoke your offer of admission.

May of senior year:

- May 1 is the final date to make your decision about where you will enroll. Get the commitment forms to your college on time, along with your deposit.
- Take your AP® Exams; they may earn you credit at your college.
- Deliver thank-you notes and a college decision update to your counselor and to the teachers who wrote your letters of recommendation.

June of senior year:

- Have a fun but safe graduation. You've worked too hard to let a bad decision take you down at this point.

Appendix: Foundational Knowledge Your Student Should Know

Adults who have attended college sometimes take for granted that students understand the basic terminology and organization of higher education. I find that many students appreciate clarification of some common admissions and college terms so that they clearly comprehend the details and nuances of college-based discussions. You may want to go over this list with your student to ensure they understand these basics.

PUBLIC VS. PRIVATE COLLEGES

In the U.S., colleges fall into one of two categories—public or private. Public colleges can further be divided into service academies, community colleges, state colleges, and state universities, each of which is described below.

For a link to our infographic on public vs. private colleges, visit this book's resources page at https://www.CollegePrep-Counseling.com/resources.

PUBLIC (FUNDED BY THE FEDERAL GOVERNMENT)

Only the five military service academies are fully funded by the U.S. government. Although tuition, housing, and food are fully paid for by the government while the student is in school (and they pay students a stipend while enrolled), these colleges require that the student serve a number of years in the military or in other approved employment or service after graduation. The student must also pass a physical to be eligible. These colleges are:

- U.S. Naval Academy in Annapolis, Maryland
- U.S. Military Academy in West Point, New York
- U.S. Air Force Academy in Silver Springs, Colorado
- U.S. Coast Guard Academy in New London, Connecticut
- U.S. Merchant Marine Academy in Kings Point, New York

PUBLIC (FUNDED BY THE STATES)

The vast majority of public colleges are funded by the individual states (and the taxpayers in those states). In most states, there are three levels of public colleges: community colleges, state colleges, and state universities.

COMMUNITY COLLEGES

These are public two-year colleges that normally serve students from the local community. Because most students live at home, these colleges don't usually offer on-campus housing. Students who are seeking a four-year bachelor's degree (what most people think of when they say, "college degree") will need to transfer to a four-year college to complete the final two years. Some examples:

> Borough of Manhattan Community College
> Northeast Texas Community College
> The College of the Florida Keys
> Santa Barbara City College
> Diablo Valley College

STATE COLLEGES

These are public four-year colleges that mainly serve residents from within the state. Students from other states may apply and enroll, but they will be asked to pay an extra "out-of-state resident" fee. These colleges can often be identified by the word "state" in the college name. Larger states can have many state university campuses (for example, there are 64 SUNY—or "State University of New York" campuses). Some examples:

> Salem State College (Massachusetts)
> State University of New York
> Florida State University
> Arizona State University
> Oregon State University
> Penn State University (Pennsylvania)

STATE UNIVERSITIES

Like the state colleges, these are public four-year institutions that mainly serve residents from within each state, and students from other states may need to pay an "out-of-state resident" fee if they choose to attend.

In any given state, there are usually fewer state universities than state colleges. For example, there are 23 schools in the California State system but only 10 universities in the University of California system. Usually, state universities require that a student have a higher GPA and/or test scores, making it more difficult to earn admission to a state university compared to a state college. Some examples of state universities (note the tell-tale "University of ..." naming convention):

University of Massachusetts
University of Michigan
University of Illinois
University of Washington
University of Florida
University of Arizona
University of Oregon

One notable exception to this naming rule: The University of Pennsylvania is a private, Ivy League university.

PRIVATE COLLEGES

Private colleges are not funded by any given state. Their tuition and fees are therefore the same for students who enroll regardless of whether the student resides in the same state as the college or is coming from a different state.

Private colleges are free from some of the non-discrimination rules that apply to public colleges. They can admit students who are exclusively male or exclusively female. They can limit admission to students who are of specific religious faiths, and more.

The Cost of Attendance for private colleges is, in general, higher than the cost for public colleges, but financial aid often mitigates this extra cost for families. Private colleges often have smaller population sizes than state colleges or universities. Some are even as small as high schools, with 1,500 to 2,500 students. Here are a few examples of private colleges:

> The College of Wooster
> Denison University
> Gonzaga University
> Gettysburg College
> Vanderbilt University
> Reed College
> Duke University

COLLEGE VS. UNIVERSITY

Generally speaking, a "college" is a two- or four-year school that offers mainly associate's or bachelor's degrees (and sometimes a few master's degrees). Universities offer not only bachelor's degrees but also master's degrees and doctoral degrees. Some examples:

> Dartmouth College
> Southern Methodist University
> Syracuse University
> Carleton College

WHAT DEGREE IS THE STUDENT PURSUING?

Colleges offer a variety of degrees. It's critical that applicants understand what degree they are actually seeking when applying to college.

ASSOCIATE'S DEGREES

Associate's degrees are offered by community colleges and usually take the equivalent of two years' full-time study to complete. The abbreviation for this degree is AA for Associate of Arts or AS for Associate of Science.

BACHELOR'S DEGREES

Bachelor's degrees are offered by private and public colleges and universities. They usually take the equivalent of four years' full-time study to complete.

There are different types of bachelor's degrees. These include the BA (Bachelor of Arts), BS or BSc (Bachelor of Science), and BFA (Bachelor of Fine Arts), depending on the student's main area of study. A Bachelor of Arts degree does not necessarily mean that a person studied art or painting. A student can earn a Bachelor of Arts degree in biology, history, English, philosophy, and more.

MASTER'S DEGREES

Students who have completed their bachelor's degree can continue studying for another year (or more) to earn a higher-level degree called a master's degree. Master's degrees follow the same format as bachelor's degrees in that they can be awarded as a

Master of Arts (MA), Master of Science (MS or MSc), Master of Fine Arts (MFA), and so on.

DOCTORAL DEGREE (OR "TERMINAL" DEGREE)

The highest degree a student can earn—also called a "terminal" degree as it's the final, or end, degree that can be earned—is the doctoral degree. The most common is the Doctor of Philosophy degree, or Ph.D., which is awarded to those who study English, history, biology, chemistry, and a variety of other academic subjects. The Juris Doctor, or J.D., is awarded to those who have graduated from law school. And an M.D., or Medical Doctorate degree, is for those who have graduated from medical school.

NAMING THE COLLEGE YEARS

High school students are familiar with how we name each of the four years of high school—freshman, sophomore, junior, senior. A few are surprised to learn that the same naming applies to each of the four years of college—freshman, sophomore, junior, and senior.

MORE TERMINOLOGY: UNDERGRADUATE, GRADUATE, POST-DOC

Students who are in their first four years of college are called "undergraduates," that is, they have not yet graduated from college. Students working toward a Master's Degree, Ph.D., or other terminal degrees are called "graduate students."

Students who have recently finished their terminal degrees but are still working at a university and/or doing research are often called "post-docs" because it is a time after, or "post," their doctoral degree.

Afterword

I'd like to thank you not only for taking the time to read through this book—I hope you've found it helpful!—but also for caring enough about your student and their future that you are putting in the time and energy to help them through this process.

If you have one more moment, I'd greatly appreciate your feedback on what was most helpful for you and what you would have liked me to add or explain in more depth. I'll take that information into consideration for the second edition. Please send that to my email address: Beth@CollegePrepCounseling.com.

Best of luck to you and your student in this process!

Beth Pickett